NEW YORK

▪ MEMORIES OF TIMES PAST ▪

▪ 60 PAINTINGS BY FREDERICK CHILDE HASSAM,
WILLIAM LOUIS SONNTAG JR.,
WILLIAM MERRITT CHASE,
AND COLIN CAMPBELL COOPER ▪

WRITTEN BY FRANCIS MORRONE

Thunder Bay Press
An imprint of the Advantage Publishers Group
10350 Barnes Canyon Road, San Diego, CA 92121
www.thunderbaybooks.com

All notations of errors or omissions should be addressed to Thunder Bay Press,
Editorial Department, at the above address. All other correspondence (author inquiries,
permissions) concerning the content of this book should be addressed to
Worth Press Ltd, Cambridge, United Kingdom. www.worthpress.co.uk

ISBN-13: 978-1-59223-868-2
ISBN-10: 1-59223-868-8

Library of Congress Cataloging-in-Publication Data

Morrone, Francis, 1958–
Memories of times past : New York / 60 paintings by Frederick
Childe Hassam … [et al.] ; written by Francis Morrone.
p. cm.
Includes bibliographical references.
ISBN 978-1-59223-868-2
1. New York (N.Y.)—In art. 2. Painting, American—20th century.
3. New York (N.Y.)—History. I. Title.
ND1460.N48M67 2008
759.147'1—dc22   2007048973

Project manager   John Button
Design manager   Lucy Guenot

Set in Centaur and Gill Sans by Bookcraft Ltd, Stroud, Gloucestershire, United Kingdom

1 2 3 4 5 12 11 10 09 08

Printed in China by Imago

A NOTE TO THE READER
In order to keep the pages of the book as uncluttered as possible,
all sources, notes, and captions relating to illustrations other than
the main paintings have been grouped at the end of the book, and
will be found on pages 171–174.

The front endpaper is taken from a large paper bird's-eye view
map of New York published by August R. Ohman & Co. in 1907.
The back endpaper is from Hammond's *Atlas of New York City and
the Metropolitan District* of 1908.

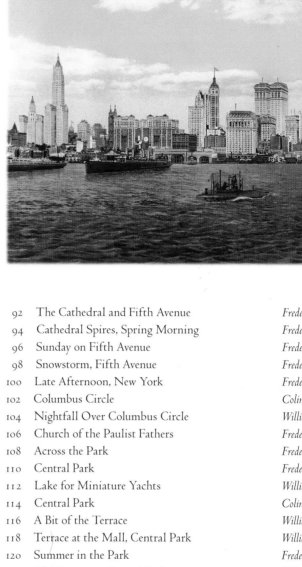

CONTENTS

Fifty Glimpses of New York
from Original Photographs

MERCANTILE ILLUSTRATING Co.

NEW YORK
THE WONDER CITY

BROOKLYN BRIDGE

NEW YORK 1910

FRANCIS MORRONE

THE IMMIGRANT CITY

Great cities are places of vivid contrasts. New York in 1910 was most definitely a place of contrasts. That period gave us the most majestic architecture the city has known—and a Lower East Side that was probably the most humanly overcrowded district on earth. That district pulsated with working-class life, and pushcart vendors hawking their wares made a perpetual street-market of the neighborhood. Since Manhattan has no back alleys, garbage is put out in front of buildings. With so many people crowded into tenements, mounds of refuse tumbled into the streets. By 1910, automobiles had appeared in New York, but people didn't see them in the poorer districts. Instead, horses continued to tread the Lower East Side, adding to the jumble—and the stench.

Who were the denizens of the most overcrowded district on earth? They were mostly European peasants. New York has experienced several great waves of immigration. In the 1840s and 1850s, Irish and Germans engulfed the city. In 1855, nearly a third of all New Yorkers had been born in Ireland. By 1910, the Irish had largely overcome the desperate poverty in which they had lived after coming to New York. They rose by infiltrating, then largely controlling, the city's government. The Irish cop on the beat may seem a Hollywood cliché, but he was also a reality. The police force was overwhelmingly Irish, and the Irish also had a lock on New York's Democratic Party, the fabled Tammany Hall machine that by 1910 had run the city for half a century.

Around 1890, new immigrants arrived, including Italians and Russian Jews. The Italian part of the Lower East Side was called "Little Italy"; the rest of the Lower East Side became overwhelmingly Jewish. The intensive immigration of these groups took place between 1890 and 1924, until the U.S. Congress passed the National Origins Act in 1924,

Sidewalk haberdasher, Lower East Side, Manhattan, photograph by William Henry Jackson/Detroit Photographic Company, 1904 (above); New York ghetto, drawing by Henry Mayer from *The Real New York*, 1904 (far left); the policeman (left) is also by Henry Mayer.

Italian women selling bread in Manhattan, a 1900 photochrome (top right); Ellis Island immigrant station, *King's Views of New York City*, 1893 (top left); immigrants in New York, *United States Pictures*, 1891 (top center); cover of *The Real New York*, 1904 (bottom).

effectively enacting a moratorium on mass immigration into the country. The law would be finally repealed in 1965.

At first, few Italians intended to stay in New York. The immigrants were mostly men who had temporarily left their families to come to America to work and save money so they could buy a plot of land and enjoy a better life back in Italy. In fact, many Italians did return to Italy, but many stayed and arranged for their families to join them in New York.

The Jews of Eastern Europe, on the other hand, had no fantasies of returning. They had left to escape the pogroms. They richly exploited the city's educational opportunities, making the most of the public schools en route to careers in the learned professions. Typically, Jewish students' teachers were Irish women—a charming fact, demonstrating how one immigrant group aided the ascent of a later group.

THE GOLDEN CITY

As masses of recent immigrants lived in poverty, upper-class New Yorkers were richer and more numerous than ever. It was the age of the nouveaux riches, industrial millionaires and financial manipulators whom journalists labeled "robber barons." While some were indeed crooks, the term "robber baron" has been much too broadly applied, and there was also much philanthropy.

Emblematic of the age were the Vanderbilts. Cornelius Vanderbilt was born in poverty in 1793. Barely literate, he became the hardest-working steamboat pilot on the New York waterways, eventually building a steamboat empire that made him rich. In the 1860s he became serious about railroads, merging several lines to form the mighty New York Central. He was a rough man, given to cursing, and not afraid to beat his competitors with his fists. Such an uncouth man could not possibly enter society.

The aristocratic old guard of New York prided itself on lineages dating back to the Dutch and English beginnings of the city. The social elite was based on inherited wealth, polite manners, and daunting social protocol. It is vividly depicted in Edith Wharton's

novel *The Age of Innocence*, set in the 1870s. Cornelius Vanderbilt, who died in 1877, would neither have fit in at a dinner party in Wharton's novel, nor would he have wanted to. When he died, he was the richest man in America.

The "Commodore," as he was known, left almost his entire estate to his son William Henry Vanderbilt. William was hardworking, stodgy, and did not aspire to social success. The Commodore's grandchildren, however, were different. Their assault upon the social citadel is the stuff of New York legend. The family that reigned above all others in social New York was the Astors. Mrs. William Astor lived in a brownstone mansion at Fifth Avenue and Thirty-fourth Street. Once a year she hosted a ball that was the most important social event of the season. Her ballroom purportedly held four hundred people. Since you could not count yourself in society unless Mrs. Astor invited you to her ball, then, as a simple matter of logic, no more than four hundred people could at any time be in society. Throughout America, the term "the Four Hundred" has ever since been a synonym for high society.

Mrs. Astor loathed the Vanderbilts, but it proved ultimately futile to hold out against them. In 1883, Alva

From top left: Cornelius Vanderbilt; William Kissam Vanderbilt; Mrs. William Astor, photographed by Carolus-Duran in 1896 (all in the New York Public Library collection). The 1905 postcard (top right) shows the Vanderbilt residences looking north from Fifty-first Street, with St. Thomas Episcopal Church and Fifth Avenue Presbyterian Church. The fan is a color photograph from the *Graphic Arts and Crafts Yearbook* from 1907.

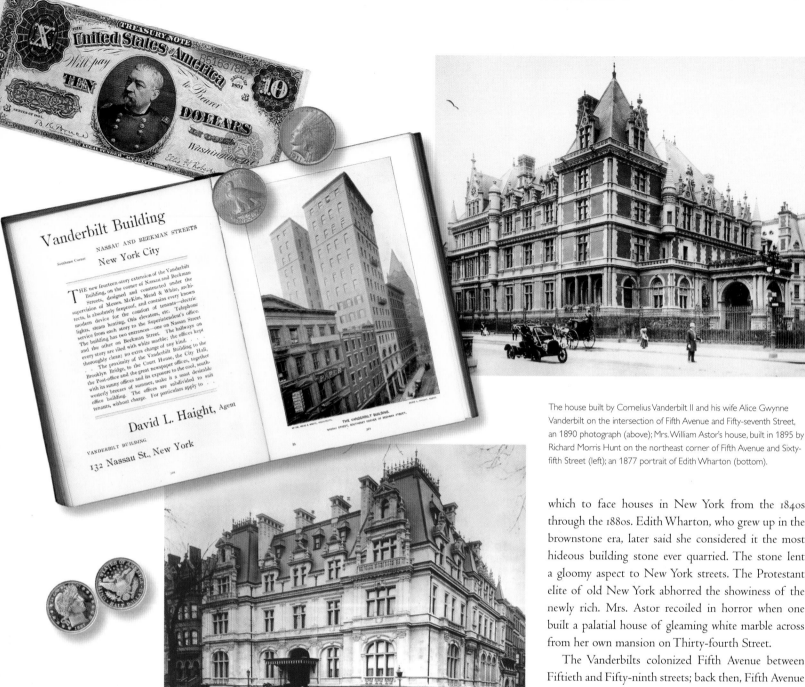

Vanderbilt Building

NASSAU AND BEEKMAN STREETS

Southern Corner

New York City

THE new fourteen-story extension of the Vanderbilt Building, on the corner of Nassau and Beekman Streets, designed and constructed under the supervision of Messrs. McKim, Mead & White, architects, is absolutely fireproof, and contains every known modern device for the comfort of tenants—electric lights, steam heating, Otis elevators, etc. Telephone service from each story to the Superintendent's office. The building has two entrances—one on Nassau Street and the other on Beekman Street. The hallways on every story are tiled with white marble; the offices kept thoroughly clean; no extra charge of any kind.

The proximity of the Vanderbilt Building to the Brooklyn Bridge, to the Court House, the City Hall, the Post-office and the great newspaper offices, together with its sunny offices and its exposure to the cool, south-westerly breezes of summer, make it a most desirable office building. The offices are subdivided to suit tenants, without charge. For particulars apply to

David L. Haight, Agent

VANDERBILT BUILDING

132 Nassau St., New York

The house built by Cornelius Vanderbilt II and his wife Alice Gwynne Vanderbilt on the intersection of Fifth Avenue and Fifty-seventh Street, an 1890 photograph (above); Mrs. William Astor's house, built in 1895 by Richard Morris Hunt on the northeast corner of Fifth Avenue and Sixty-fifth Street (left); an 1877 portrait of Edith Wharton (bottom).

which to face houses in New York from the 1840s through the 1880s. Edith Wharton, who grew up in the brownstone era, later said she considered it the most hideous building stone ever quarried. The stone lent a gloomy aspect to New York streets. The Protestant elite of old New York abhorred the showiness of the newly rich. Mrs. Astor recoiled in horror when one built a palatial house of gleaming white marble across from her own mansion on Thirty-fourth Street.

The Vanderbilts colonized Fifth Avenue between Fiftieth and Fifty-ninth streets; back then, Fifth Avenue was a street of private mansions, not of commerce as it is today. At first the Vanderbilt houses were as dreary-looking as anything else in New York. Soon, however, the Vanderbilts made showiness socially acceptable, and New York was never the same.

Cornelius Vanderbilt II, the Commodore's grandson, built a spectacular mansion on Fifth Avenue between Fifty-seventh and Fifty-eighth streets, in the style of a Loire Valley château. Shortly thereafter, the Vanderbilts helped build up a new neighborhood of the rich, the Upper East Side, in the blocks east of Central Park. That neighborhood, flourishing by 1910,

Vanderbilt, wife of the Commodore's grandson William Kissam Vanderbilt, held a ball to rival Mrs. Astor's. When prominent New Yorkers, including members of the Four Hundred—and Mrs. Astor's own daughter—accepted invitations, Mrs. Astor knew the jig was up. The Vanderbilts were then admitted to society.

Mrs. Astor's mansion was faced in a muddy sandstone, or brownstone, the accepted material with

The Metropolitan Club (also known as "the Millionaires' Club"), from *King's Views* of 1893 (above); "Wild West at Madison Square Garden," a 1903 poster, and a Garden Theater program from 1891 (top right); Madison Square Garden from *New York: Wonder City*, of about 1919.

has ever since remained the domicile of the richest families in America.

The architects who by 1910 had definitively repudiated the Victorian era of dreary brownstone were McKim, Mead & White. From the 1880s to the 1910s, the firm led the way in giving to New York a classical splendor to rival Paris, Vienna, Rome, St. Petersburg, and Dublin.

Stanford White was both a great architect and one of the flamboyant characters of "Gilded Age" New York. He designed the Metropolitan Club, an imposing Renaissance-style private club at Fifth Avenue and Sixtieth Street. Its interiors were among the city's most opulent. The club was founded by financier J. P. Morgan. Legend has it that when Morgan was a member of the Union Club, the city's most exclusive, he got upset when some of his business colleagues were denied membership—so he formed his own club. Wealth, not social pedigree, was the common denominator of the club's membership. Thus, unsurprisingly, it also became the club of the Vanderbilts.

Bird's-eye View of the P. R. R. Depot, New York.

Two postcards of Pennsylvania Station (above); a 1903 postcard of Evelyn Nesbit Thaw (below).

EVELYN NESBIT THAW
"IN A REVERIE"

White's most legendary building was Madison Square Garden, the second of four New York buildings to bear that name. It stood from the 1880s to the 1920s on Madison Avenue and Twenty-sixth Street. This lavish pleasure palace contained a vast amphitheater, a concert hall, and restaurants, and was used for sporting events, exhibitions, the National Horse Show, and conventions. The style of the building was Spanish Renaissance, and White designed a high tower patterned on the Giralda of the Cathedral of Seville. The tower contained apartments.

White is better known today as an architect than as the quintessential playboy of his era. Though he was married with a child, his wife resided year-round in a country house on eastern Long Island. White joined her on weekends. During the week, he lived a bachelor's life in the city, replete with adulterous liaisons. Most infamously, he took as his mistress a beautiful chorus girl named Evelyn Nesbit, only sixteen years old when she met White. After some time, their relationship dissolved, and Evelyn married a millionaire named Harry Thaw.

Thaw, who was the archetypal obsessive, included Stanford White among the objects of his obsession. On the night of June 25, 1906, White descended from his apartment in the tower of Madison Square Garden to the roof garden of the building. In those days before air-conditioning, summertime entertainment took place alfresco, on roofs designed for the purpose. The maître d' seated White at his customary table. Unbeknownst to White, across the floor sat Nesbit and Thaw. As the stage show went on, Thaw walked

over to White. Thaw said, "You'll never go out with that woman again." He pulled a revolver from under his coat and fired three shots into White, killing him instantly. The singers onstage had just finished "I Could Love a Thousand Girls."

White's partner, Charles McKim, was more sober. He was especially adept at large-scale projects, like the campus of Columbia University, laid out in the 1890s. His most famous work was Pennsylvania Station, flagship of America's largest passenger railroad. The station opened in 1910, a vast, granite-clad edifice of classical grandeur to rival ancient Rome. In fact, the waiting room was modeled on the baths of Caracalla.

By 1910, lightly colored materials—marble, granite, pale terra-cotta—had replaced brownstone. Above all, Indiana limestone dominated Manhattan. Architects had finally perceived that New York, a city on the latitude of Rome, has as brilliant light and as beautiful skies as to be found anywhere on earth. Indiana limestone, when in shade, may appear dingy like cement, but in direct light it gleams, shimmers, and bursts forth in a thousand kaleidoscopic colors.

By 1910, New York shimmered.

SHOPPING AND NIGHTLIFE

By 1910, New York merchants had made available to the masses the greatest possible variety of consumer goods. New York, arguably, invented the department store, though many presume Paris to have done so. Paris did once have the biggest dry-goods stores in the world, but they had not crossed the line to become full-fledged department stores. In 1846, New York's greatest merchant, the Irish immigrant A. T. Stewart, opened the city's largest dry-goods emporium, the "Marble Palace," on Broadway

Lord & Taylor's Grand Street dry-goods establishment at Chrystie Street, from *King's Views* of 1893 (above); postcards of the Twenty-third Street shopping district and the Municipal Building at night (top).

THE CZAR OF THE DEPARTMENT STORE

Postcard of the Siegel-Cooper department store and Edward Morrison & Son's store from *King's Views* (top); Siegel-Cooper advertisement from 1910 (above); "The Czar of the Department Store" by Henry Mayer, from *The Real New York*, 1904 (right).

and Reade Street. In 1862 he moved uptown, to Broadway and Tenth Street, where he built a vast cast-iron edifice known as "Stewart's New Store." This was the first department store in the modern sense, a store that sold everything to outfit a life from cribs to coffins. By 1910 the store still flourished, though it had changed ownership and had been renamed Wanamaker's.

After Stewart's move, rival merchants built stores even farther uptown. Old New York retailers Arnold Constable and Lord & Taylor opened north along Broadway. The line of department stores turned west at Twenty-third Street, where one found Stern Brothers and McCreery's. Then the line turned south on Sixth Avenue. Adams Dry Goods, Hugh O'Neill's, Simpson-Crawford, Altman's, and Macy's all called Sixth Avenue home. But the grandest of all was Siegel-Cooper, occupying the full block of Sixth Avenue between Eighteenth and Nineteenth streets. The opulent store,

The Metropolitan Opera House, from *The Best and Latest Photographs of Greater New York* by Isaac H. Blanchard, 1899 (above); a color advertisement card for Tiffany's (above right); a 1910 postcard of the Waldorf-Astoria Hotel (right); and the Gorham Manufacturing Company on Broadway at the northwest corner of Nineteenth Street, from *King's Views* of 1893 (bottom right).

which sold everything under the sun and offered all the amenities required for a full day's pleasurable outing in sumptuous surroundings, billed itself as the largest store in the world. The elaborate building still stands, though Siegel-Cooper did not survive World War I.

The department-store loop was known as "Ladies' Mile." By 1910, however, stores had begun to move farther uptown. Macy's was the first, moving in 1902 from Sixth Avenue and Fourteenth Street to Broadway and Thirty-fourth Street. Macy's now claimed that it, not Siegel-Cooper, was the world's largest store. Later that year, Saks & Company opened across from Macy's on Thirty-fourth Street. A block away, Altman's moved in 1906 from Sixth Avenue and Eighteenth Street to Fifth Avenue and Thirty-fourth Street, diagonally across the avenue from the city's most celebrated hotel, the Waldorf-Astoria, built in the 1890s by the Astors, on the site of two Astor mansions. Later, the Empire State Building replaced the hotel on the site, and the Waldorf moved to Park Avenue.

Elegant specialty shops started to open on the once-staunchly residential Fifth Avenue. Tiffany's, which

began in 1837, moved in 1906 into a splendid Venetian Renaissance-style building that Stanford White designed on Fifth Avenue and Thirty-seventh Street. One block south, White designed a new building for Gorham, the high-class metalsmiths. White's elegant stores were called "retail palazzos," designed to look as though they were private mansions rather than commercial premises.

New York had long been a theatrical center. In the early nineteenth century, theaters clustered along the Bowery. Later, Union Square at Fourteenth Street was the theatrical neighborhood. At the time of Edith Wharton's *The Age of Innocence*, the city's opera house was the Academy of Music, on Fourteenth Street east of Union Square. There, New York's old-guard society went not so much to hear opera but to see and be seen. When nouveaux riches wanted in on the fun, they found the house was too small and no boxes were for sale. So in 1883, new money built a rival house, the Metropolitan Opera House, on Broadway and

The New York Times Building, from *New York: Wonder City*, 1919 (left); advertisement for White Rock Water at Times Square on the Great White Way, a postcard of 1913 (above left); a 1913 postcard of the Metropolitan Life Building at night (above right).

Thirty-eighth Street. The "Met" led to the Broadway and Thirty-fourth Street neighborhood becoming the new theatrical district. After department stores horned in on the neighborhood, the theaters fled uptown to Forty-second Street, and to points north, to Fifty-ninth Street along the Broadway spine. Prior to 1904, the neighborhood of Broadway and Forty-second Street was known as Longacre Square, and was the center of carriage manufacturing.

In 1904, the *New York Times* moved from "Newspaper Row," downtown near City Hall, to the triangular plot formed by Broadway's diagonal intersection with north-south Seventh Avenue at Forty-second Street. This would become known as Times Square. The first New Year's Eve ball drop from the Times Tower took place on December 31, 1904. As theaters massed around Times Square, the area glowed at night with electrically illuminated advertising signs. Colorful neon had yet to be invented, so the glow was the white glow of thousands of incandescent bulbs, earning this stretch of Broadway the nickname "the Great White Way."

New York Harbor at Night.

URBAN TECHNOLOGY

By 1910 much of New York's modern infrastructure was in place. Electric illumination had replaced gas lighting. The city's subterranean electric railroad—the subway—was in operation. The telephone was ubiquitous. Automobiles mixed with horses on the streets.

Above all, the skyscraper age had dawned. Before the 1890s, buildings were built much as they had ever been. The higher a building, the thicker its external walls had to be to support the added weight. This placed a natural limitation on how high buildings could rise—at some point, the walls in the lower part of the building would become so thick there would be no room for lobbies, elevators, or stores. This changed in the 1890s. Engineers perfected the internal framework of steel columns and beams, freeing external walls from supporting the building. Such walls became, in effect, material draped on steel frameworks—hence the architect's term "curtain wall." New York built one building after another that claimed the title of world's tallest. In 1910 the tallest building in the world stood on the southeast corner of Madison Avenue and Twenty-fourth Street. The Metropolitan Life Insurance Company Building was fifty stories high, distinctively patterned after the Campanile di San Marco in Venice. In 1910 plans were drawn up for a much taller structure, the Woolworth Building, headquarters of the global empire of five-and-dime variety stores. With an elaborate sheathing of Gothic details rendered in gleaming white-glazed terra-cotta, the Woolworth Building opened in 1913, shooting 792 feet in the air.

By 1910 New York had become what it would remain for half a century: a city that looked like no other the world had ever known. The buildings rose higher than they did anywhere else; the bridges spanned greater distances. Of all the world's cities besides New York, only Chicago had clusters of tall buildings. For anyone visiting New York, especially the immigrants arriving at Ellis Island, the city presented an awesome sight—a scene of such technological grandeur that one would have had to go back to the gild-encrusted Constantinople of the Middle Ages to find another city that seemed to pilgrims from afar as though it must be a fantasy.

Perhaps the truest measure of New York at the time came in 1912, in a book by the English novelist Arnold Bennett. In *Your United States*, Bennett wrote of the Bronx, a borough then being intensively developed. It was a wholly new place, intended for immigrants or immigrant progeny who had made the trek from the Lower East Side. Bennett said there was no place on earth, nor had there ever been, with a higher general standard of living than the Bronx, where all the new apartments boasted hot water, central heat, electricity, and the most modern plumbing. The Bronx, Bennett said, was "a wondrous sign of the essential vigor of American civilization." It was as close as mankind had yet come to Utopia.

A 1910 postcard of New York Harbor at night (top left); a 1900 photochrome of the thirty-story Park Row Building, the world's tallest from 1899 to 1908 (top right); a 1910 postcard of the Woolworth Building at night (above).

FREDERICK CHILDE HASSAM
1859–1935

Self-portrait, 1914 (above); *Country Road*, watercolor, 1882 (right).

Childe Hassam was arguably as great a painter as America has produced. Paul Johnson has called Hassam "the outstanding cityscape painter of the modern age." His city was New York.

Frederick Childe Hassam was born in 1859 in Dorchester, now part of Boston, Massachusetts. His father, Frederick Hassam, was an antiques dealer, and the family was of old New England Puritan stock. Childe left high school after only a year to go to work. He worked briefly in the famous Boston publishing firm of Little, Brown, where he failed in the accounting department. His supervisor, however, noticed the boy's

facility in drawing, and encouraged him to pursue an artistic career. In 1876 Hassam became apprenticed to a wood engraver, and after a few years established his own engraving business in Boston. Meanwhile, he had also achieved success as a commercial illustrator, his works appearing in such magazines as *Harper's*, *Scribner's*, and *Century*—the leading periodicals of the day. He also found work as a book illustrator.

All the while he took classes in painting and drawing, most notably from the renowned American sculptor and painter William Rimmer. Watercolor became Hassam's forte, and in 1882 he had his first solo

The Room of Flowers, 1894.

exhibition, in Boston, featuring some fifty watercolors, principally of beach scenes on Nantucket.

The following year he made his first trip abroad, traveling throughout Britain and the Continent. In England, he was captivated by J. M. W. Turner's works, which would prove a potent influence on Hassam. Upon his return to Boston, he had a second solo exhibition, this time of his European watercolors.

In the year of that exhibition, 1884, he married Kathleen Maud Doane. The couple bore no children. Living in Boston, he began to make watercolors of Boston scenes, beginning his great career as a cityscape artist. He loved to depict the city through mist, and at night, and concentrated on the movement of pedestrians and carriages. He wished to be—to use Baudelaire's phrase—"the painter of modern life." Even

so, he felt he lacked certain technical skills, particularly in the all-important depiction of the human figure, and to remedy this, he returned to Europe in 1886 to study at the Académie Julian in Paris. He wished to acquire a strong background of academic skills, though he in no way wished to paint academic pictures. His teachers were the formidable Gustave Boulanger (one of the decorators of the Paris Opera House) and Jules-Joseph Lefebvre (famous for his nudes and renowned as a teacher).

In 1887 one of Hassam's Parisian cityscape paintings was exhibited at the Salon—a high accomplishment. In 1888 he ceased his studies at the Académie but remained in Paris with his wife. He adored Paris—the "City of Light," the most captivating of the world's great cities. Most importantly, Hassam saw and reveled

Auction advertisement from the *New York Times*, February 6, 1896 (above); *Newfields, New Hampshire*, etching and drypoint, 1916 (below); *Pont-Aven, Noonday*, 1897 (opposite).

in the works of the Impressionists. At this time, he would have seen works by Monet, Degas, Renoir, Pissarro, Seurat, Cézanne, Gauguin, and the American Mary Cassatt. A headier time and place for a young artist is hard to imagine. Henceforth Hassam was seen as an "American Impressionist."

In 1889 Hassam and his wife returned to the United States, settling in New York, which had become the premier marketplace for art in the country. He found New York inspiring. The city's swirl of motion and the strong light, as beautiful as any in the world, stirred Hassam to create a veritable catalog of the 1890s city. He had his first solo show in the city at the American Art Galleries at Madison Square in 1896. In 1897 Hassam and his close friends J. Alden Weir and John Henry Twachtman formed a group known as the "Ten American Painters" in opposition to New York's

established artists' institutions, the National Academy of Design and the Society of American Artists, which was once progressive but was becoming more conservative. The other members of the "Ten" were Frank W. Benson, Joseph De Camp, Thomas Wilmer Dewing, Willard Leroy Metcalf, Robert Reid, Edward Simmons, and Edmund Tarbell. Winslow Homer declined an invitation to join.

The following year the Ten held an exhibition at the city's Durand-Ruel Gallery. A principal goal of the Ten was to change the way exhibitions were mounted; instead of gallery walls crowded with paintings, the Ten demanded that enough space be given to each painting for it to be properly contemplated. The group exhibited together until 1918. When Twachtman died in 1902, he was replaced by William Merritt Chase. The group's independent spirit is said to have paved the way for New York's important Armory Show of 1913, in which modern American and European artists, including Cézanne, Picasso, and Duchamp, altered the American artistic landscape for many decades to come. Hassam exhibited at the Armory Show, but forswore the more extreme modern art on display. To make ends meet, Hassam neither taught nor painted portraits, but rather worked as a book illustrator, as he had since the earliest years of his career. A notable example is his illustrations for *Venetian Life* by William Dean Howells.

In 1910 Hassam returned to Paris, where in that year he produced his first "flag painting." City streets festooned with billowing flags hanging from buildings captivated Hassam, providing a rich opportunity to capture complex motion and light. He was in heaven when—between 1916 and 1919, both to rally for war and then to celebrate its end—flags flew everywhere, in Paris, in London, and especially in New York, where Hassam considered his flag paintings his proudest achievement. In the later years of his career Hassam circled back to his beginnings as an artist, concentrating on printmaking. He spent his summers in an eighteenth-century farmhouse in East Hampton, on the far eastern end of Long Island. It was there that Hassam died in 1935.

WILLIAM MERRITT CHASE
1849–1916

Like Hassam's, William Merritt Chase's beginnings were unprepossessing. Born in a small town in Indiana, he grew up in Indianapolis, where amid desultory schooling he worked in his father's shoe store. He showed artistic talent, and at seventeen began to take lessons from local artists. Eager to leave Indianapolis, which he found boring, he joined the U.S. Navy, which he found even less tolerable than Indianapolis. He finagled a discharge and moved to New York City to study at the National Academy of Design. He was in New York in 1869–70 before rejoining his parents, who had moved to St. Louis, Missouri.

In St. Louis, Chase established a studio, where he made a living painting commissioned portraits and still lifes. From 1872 to 1877 he lived in Munich, where he joined an American community of artists studying at the Royal Academy. These included Henry James's friend Frank Duveneck, and John Henry Twachtman, who would become Childe Hassam's close friend. The "Munich technique" was derived essentially from the Spanish master Diego Velázquez and the Dutch master Frans Hals. The Munich teachers emphasized large-scale history paintings executed in a bravura manner with bold brushstrokes. Chase's teacher was the renowned history painter Karl von Piloty.

Chase rejected history painting for more intimate subjects, but rendered those subjects in a manner deeply influenced by Piloty. In 1877 Chase, Duveneck, and Twachtman went to live in Venice, where Chase's palette turned much brighter than that of the Munich painters. The following year he moved to New York. With five years of intensive Munich training under his belt, he obtained a job as an instructor at the Art Students League. He became a member of the Society of American Artists, a progressive organization that

Self-portrait: The Artist in his Studio, 1916 (top);
A Stormy Day, Bath Beach, 1888 (opposite top);
A Sunny Day at Shinnecock Bay, 1892 (opposite bottom).

rebelled against the stuffy National Academy. The Society of American Artists, in turn, became more conservative, giving rise to the group calling itself the "Ten American Painters," founded by Childe Hassam and Chase's friend Twachtman, and of which Chase himself would become a member.

Chase served as president of the Society of American Artists in 1880, and from 1885 to 1895. At the Art Students League, he won a devoted following among students, especially female students whose careers he helped to promote. His pedagogy stressed "direct painting," the direct application of a fully loaded brush to the canvas without prior drawing. Chase was more influential as a teacher than as an artist. Through his teaching and his extensive membership in formal and informal artists' organizations, he became recognized as a leader of the New York art world.

Throughout this period, extending to 1895, Chase moved ever further from the Munich model, assimilating the techniques of the Impressionists. His paintings were

In 1886 he married one of his models, Alice Brémond Gerson. They had eight children—which will put a crimp in anyone's flamboyant lifestyle. For a while the Chases lived with Alice's parents in Bedford-Stuyvesant, Brooklyn, at the time a new, genteel neighborhood of handsome houses and much greenery. This is when Chase made his famous Brooklyn paintings, including memorable images of Prospect Park, Tompkins Park, Coney Island, Bath Beach, the Navy Yard, and his own backyard. He also painted Central Park in Manhattan, and the seafront at Shinnecock, at the eastern end of Long Island, near East Hampton—to where Childe Hassam retreated in his later years.

Among the students taught by Chase at the Art Students League or the Brooklyn Art Association were Rockwell Kent, Georgia O'Keeffe, Charles Sheeler, Charles Demuth, Edward Hopper, Marsden Hartley, Howard Chandler Christy, and Joseph Stella, several of whom went on to become more famous than their teacher. In 1896 he formed his own school in New York, the Chase School of Art. For all the progressivism that he inspired in his students, Chase, like Hassam, deplored the Armory Show in 1913. Neither man could abide what they viewed as the poor technical skills of many modern painters. Chase died in 1916.

very popular among buyers. He set up a studio in the Tenth Street Studio Building in Greenwich Village. This building had been designed and built by the architect Richard Morris Hunt in the 1860s. Hunt had been the first American to enroll in the École des Beaux-Arts in Paris, and he wished to recreate the École's atmosphere in New York. Hunt housed his own wildly successful architectural firm (among his credits is the Metropolitan Museum of Art in New York) in the Studio Building, and ran his firm as though it were an École des Beaux-Arts atelier, training a generation of American architects. In addition, many painters took up residence in the building, as Hunt felt it was essential for architects and artists to work in close proximity to each other. Among these painters were Winslow Homer, Frederic Church, and John La Farge.

But of all the artists who made their homes in the Studio Building, arguably none did so with Chase's impact. He was considered quite a character. He stuffed his studio with an improbable collection of objets d'art and bric-a-brac culled from around the world and all historical periods. His African American manservant dressed in Turkish costume as Chase entertained clients in an atmosphere of object-laden bohemianism and luxury. Soon Chase became more famous for his flamboyant lifestyle—the subject of newspaper and magazine articles—than for either his art or his teaching.

COLIN CAMPBELL COOPER
1856–1937

Self-portrait, 1922 (above); *Dordrecht Harbor*, 1898 (right).

Colin Campbell Cooper was born on March 8, 1856, in Philadelphia, Pennsylvania, the son of a physician with the same name. "I was brought up in Belmont, near Philadelphia," he wrote as a young man, "in a fine old Colonial manor house, with its quaint old barn dating about 1800." His father encouraged him to follow his heart, so he studied painting at the Pennsylvania Academy of the Fine Arts, the oldest art school in the United States, where he studied under Thomas Eakins, and then began studies at the Académie Julian in Paris in 1886. From 1895 to 1898 he taught watercolor at the Drexel Institute in Philadelphia.

Cooper specialized in cityscapes, documenting the modern cities of his time, both in Europe and America, beginning with Philadelphia and moving on to New York. He was one of the first painters to make skyscrapers an integral part of his subject matter. In 1897 he married the painter Emma Lampert, and the following year the couple moved to New York, where he worked out of the landmark Gainsborough Studios building at 222 Central Park South. When Emma died in 1920, Cooper moved to Santa Barbara, California.

In 1927 he married Marie Frehsee of Santa Barbara, but neither marriage produced children. He was named dean of the School of Painting at the Santa Barbara School of the Arts, and was an elder statesman of the artists' colony that formed in Santa Barbara. It was in that city that he died at the age of eighty-one.

In 1907 Cooper was among the thirty-three out of thirty-six nominees who were rejected for membership election to New York's prestigious National Academy of Design—an event that started a feud between the progressives and the conservatives, and resulted in painter Robert Henri's call for the progressives to leave the staid academy and hold their own exhibitions. From these progressives emerged the group that would put together the legendary "Armory Show" of 1913 at New York's sixty-ninth Regiment Armory. Other painters excluded in 1907 were Arthur B. Davies, Charles W. Hawthorne, Ernest Lawson, Willard Metcalf, Jerome Myers, and Albert Sterner. Cooper was in pretty good company.

In 1911 the *New York Times* noted, "For of late years we have been waking up to the fact that, from an artistic point of view, this metropolis of ours is anything but ugly. We were taught formerly to believe—and most of us, with exceeding docility, agreed to believe—that the prettiest spot in New York was an outward bound transatlantic liner." With that opening, the newspaper then asked twelve artists, "What is the prettiest spot in New York?"

The article went on to note that "first and foremost in enthusiasm for the modern New York of today, the city of towering skyscrapers and fevered street traffic, is Colin Campbell Cooper, who may be considered the skyscraper artist par excellence of America, since no man has done as much as he to win a place in art for these giant structures. Years ago Mr. Cooper became fascinated by ultra-modern life and he has stuck to his first love through thick and thin."

An inveterate traveler, in 1913 Cooper was aboard the S.S. *Carpathia* when it came to the rescue of the survivors of the *Titanic*. He helped in the rescue, and made watercolors of the event. That same year, he was elected to membership of the National Academy of Design, and the following year he visited India for the first time.

In 1931 art critic Eleanor Jewett of the *Chicago Daily Tribune* reviewed a Cooper exhibition, writing: "There

Kanchenjunga, the Himalayas, 1914 (above);
Maharaja's Palace, Jaipur, 1917 (right).

are many of us who still prefer our exhibits seasoned with craftsmanship and warm with beauty, and for those of us this is a welcome show. Quiet, mellow, strongly sure in background, demurely glowing in color, rich in the atmosphere of many different countries, Colin Campbell Cooper offers an unusual exhibition." That show included scenes of Philadelphia, Bombay, Venice, Rouen, Santa Barbara, the Himalayas, and Brittany.

Cooper's works can be found in the collections of the Metropolitan Museum of Art, New York; the Brooklyn Museum; the National Arts Club, New York; the Cincinnati Museum of Art; the New York Historical Society; the Pennsylvania Academy of the Fine Arts, Philadelphia; and the White House in Washington, D.C.

WILLIAM LOUIS SONNTAG JR.
1869–1898

In comparison to other artists, not as much is known of William Louis Sonntag Jr. In part, this is because there is not as much to know, for he died at the shockingly young age of twenty-nine.

Sonntag was born in New York City in 1869. His father was a well-known landscape painter, associated with the Hudson River School, and he was descended from a French officer who had come to America to serve in the revolutionary army. Sonntag Jr. showed precocious talent: in 1882, when he was only thirteen, he exhibited at the National Academy of Design a watercolor of the then-new Brooklyn Bridge.

He never formally studied art, but no doubt inherited much from his father. Though known as a watercolorist, he made his living as a magazine illustrator for publications like *Ladies' Home Journal*. In 1892 he married Hattie Inglis. They had no children. His *New York Times* obituary states only that he died following "a brief illness"—no clue is given as to the cause. The elder Sonntag outlived his son by one year.

Carriage Ride, New York City, watercolor, no date (right); *Under the Bridge, Evening*, watercolor on paper, no date (below); *Sixth Avenue and Fifty-ninth Street*, ink, no date (bottom left).

PLATE 1

MANHATTAN'S MISTY SUNSET

Then, as today, the New York sunset casts fiery flares across the sky, reducing buildings to silhouettes.

At first glance, the viewer might think Childe Hassam had painted this in the 1930s, perhaps shortly before his death in 1935. The two tall buildings look remarkably like—on the left—the Bank of the Manhattan Building (built 1929) on Wall Street, and—on the right—the Cities Service Building (built 1932) on Pine Street. Yet we are credibly informed that the artist made this picture in 1911, in which case the buildings depicted are not identifiable.

The view is from Brooklyn, across the East River, which appears as a thin white horizontal line about a quarter of the way up the frame. No painter ever more adeptly captured Manhattan's lowering sun with its brilliant flashes of orange light. Never before had such cityscapes been painted, for the simple reason that such cityscapes, their skylines punctuated by unprecedentedly tall buildings, had never before existed. For Hassam, the specificity of what he rendered in this evocative painting mattered much less than the overall effect.

PLATE 2

LOWER MANHATTAN

By the early twentieth century, New York had grown to be one of the major financial centers of the world.

When Childe Hassam painted this scene, many of the buildings were new, and the picture evokes the modernity of the financial center of a thriving city. The pedimented facade on the left is the New York Stock Exchange, designed by George B. Post and completed in 1903. The cupola-topped skyscraper just behind the Stock Exchange is the Gillender Building, built in 1897 and demolished just thirteen years later to make way for the Bankers Trust Building, which remains on the site today at the northwest corner of Wall and Nassau streets.

The low pedimented building to the right of the Gillender Building was—when Hassam painted this picture—the U.S. Subtreasury Building. It had been built as the United States Custom House in 1842 on the site of Federal Hall, where George Washington took the oath of office as the first president of the United States. The building's function changed when a much larger and grander custom house was constructed on the south side of Bowling Green. The Subtreasury Building, one of the city's most important Greek Revival edifices, is today a museum called Federal Hall National Memorial.

PLATE 3

VIEW OF WALL STREET

The tall buildings of New York made the city appear as no other city in the history of the world.

Cooper's view does not show us much of Wall Street, but rather the West Side waterfront of lower Manhattan. Though the picture is not dated, we know it was made after 1913, the date of the Woolworth Building, which towers over everything else in the image. From 1913 to 1929, Cass Gilbert's Gothic-ornamented tower was the tallest building in the world. Just in front of it we see the Hudson Terminal buildings, "twin towers" designed by Clinton & Russell, and built in 1908. They would be razed in the 1960s to make way for the World Trade Center.

The fancifully topped building to the right of the Woolworth is the Municipal Building (1907–14; McKim, Mead & White). In the right foreground, the building with the green mansard roof is the ornate West Street Building (1907); like the Woolworth, it is the handiwork of Cass Gilbert. The tall building at the far right is Ernest Flagg's Singer Building (1908), which had briefly been the world's tallest building, and remains the world's tallest building ever to be demolished.

The Hudson River Terminal Buildings, New York.

PLATE 4

MOUNTAINS OF MANHATTAN

People unaccustomed to buildings rising thirty or forty stories in the sky frequently likened them to mountains.

Singer Building,
and part of Financial District

Copyright 1912 by Irving Underhill, N. Y.

Though this picture is undated, we know it was made after 1908, when the most visible—and only readily identifiable—"mountain peak" was completed: the elaborately topped Singer Building by Ernest Flagg. Cooper's view toward lower Manhattan is from the western part of Midtown, an area of factories, docks, and tenements. We see New York Harbor in the right center of the frame. At the time, Midtown had not yet received its skyline of tall buildings that today give Manhattan its two distinct clusters of skyscrapers.

Cooper beautifully captures the lower Manhattan skyline's mountainous rise into the clouds and smog of the city, and in the foreground equally adeptly captures the rust-brown dinginess of the industrial city. In 1908 the Singer Building was the tallest building in the world, though it would yield that title a year later to the Metropolitan Life Insurance Building. New York City at the beginning of the twentieth century was growing ever skyward as all the land on Manhattan island had been devoured.

NEW YORK, EAST R. & HARBOUR. (FROM BROOKLYN BRIDGE.)

THE SINGER BUILDING
FROM BROOKLYN BRIDGE
ART-LOVERS' NEW YORK — VOLLAND VIEWS

PLATE 5

CLIFFS OF MANHATTAN

In the early days of skyscrapers, the city often looked like a jagged jumble of high and low buildings.

The dominant building in the center is the Lorsch Building that stood at 35 Maiden Lane. It was built in 1895. We see how tall buildings sprouted startlingly amid low surroundings. The tall, twin-cupolaed building in the upper left is the Park Row Building of 1899, designed by R. H. Robertson. From 1899 to 1908 it was the tallest office building in the world, and was at the time of Cooper's painting the headquarters of the Interborough Rapid Transit Company that was then one year away from introducing New York City's first subway line.

The building partially visible on the right is Clinton & Russell's stately Mutual Life Insurance Company Building that stood at Nassau and Liberty streets. The earliest part of this building had gone up in the early 1880s, and it had just been added to for the last time when Cooper painted this picture.

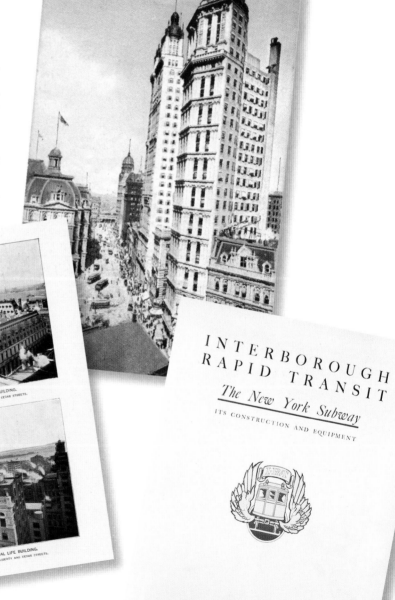

PLATE 6

OCTOBER HAZE, MANHATTAN

Some of the proudest towers on the Manhattan skyline belonged to the city's great newspapers.

This view of lower Manhattan highlights the tall buildings of "Printing House Square," the area around City Hall Park where the newspapers kept their headquarters. In the center is a dome-topped skyscraper, the New York World Building (1890, George B. Post), home to the newspaper published by the legendary Joseph Pulitzer. The building, demolished in 1955, stood next to the Brooklyn Bridge.

The pointy-topped building to its right is the New York Tribune Building (1875, Richard Morris Hunt), home of the newspaper founded by Horace Greeley, but at this time published by his protégé Whitelaw Reid, one-time American ambassador to the Court of St. James. The Tribune Building was also demolished in 1955.

The very tall building to the right is the Park Row Building (1899, R. H. Robertson), home to the Associated Press, the news-gathering consortium formed by several New York newspapers.

PLATE 7

ST. PAUL'S CHAPEL

A church that has survived great calamities, St. Paul's Chapel
is considered a landmark for many reasons.

Group of Skyscrapers, St. Paul's Chapel
and Church Yard, New York.

St. Paul's Chapel was built as an Anglican church in the 1760s, on Broadway and Vesey Street. As only a handsome, surviving Georgian edifice, it would be an honored building. But there is so much more to its history. In September 1776, after the British had forced colonial troops from the city, a fire broke out at the island's southern tip. The fire raged northward, destroying almost everything to the west of Broadway, about a third of the city's buildings. Yet the fire miraculously spared St. Paul's. It is where George and Martha Washington attended Sunday services when he served as the first president of the United States and New York was the nation's capital.

Then, in September 2001, St. Paul's somehow—again miraculously—survived the destruction of the World Trade Center, which stood immediately behind the church. The chapel is now New York's proud symbol of perseverance and survival.

A. Weingärtner's Lith? N.Y.
WASHINGTON'S PEW in ST. PAUL'S CHURCH, 1789.

PLATE 8

BROOKLYN BRIDGE IN WINTER

Before the Brooklyn Bridge was built, icy winters wreaked havoc on river crossings between Manhattan and Brooklyn.

Childe Hassam stunningly uses a limited palette of blues and whites to depict the wintry city and the graceful arc of the Brooklyn Bridge, completed in 1883, here seen soaring like a snowbird across the East River. The artist's vantage point is the Manhattan shore, south of the bridge, perhaps in the vicinity of the South Street docks. We see the Brooklyn tower of the bridge in the distance, but the snowy skies altogether obscure the borough across the river.

Only one year before this picture was painted, the Brooklyn Bridge had been eclipsed by the Williamsburg Bridge as the longest suspension bridge in the world. The Brooklyn Bridge,

however, would remain New York's most beloved. Though a feat of brute technological mastery, the bridge, as Hassam shows so well, was equally a work of art, with its powerful Gothic arches and lacelike steel-wire cables that appear diaphanous in the snowy scene.

PLATE 9

A WINTER DAY ON BROOKLYN BRIDGE

The Brooklyn Bridge eased the daily commute of Manhattan workers who walked or rode the train across the bridge.

MIDWINTER IN THE GREAT METROPOLIS.

Hassam's watercolor depicts the Manhattan tower of the bridge frontally, the proud arches of the granite tower being the symbolic portal to the wondrous city. The bridge was only nine years old when this picture was painted. Most of the streaming pedestrians have just disembarked from the steam-powered trains (as we surmise from the smoke) that had only recently been introduced on the bridge. Hassam, here as elsewhere, shows his fondness for the atmospheric effects of snow, and for subtle, tonal gradations in a narrow palette of colors. The bridge's towers rose 276 feet 6 inches above the high-water mark, making them second only to the tower of Trinity Church among the highest structures in the city.

We presume that the pedestrians moving toward us are Brooklynites going to work on this frigid morning. In 1892 Brooklyn was still a completely separate city from New York, though as the bridge, physically joining the two cities across the East River, portended, it would not be long before the two cities would become one—just six years from when Hassam painted this scene.

THE DAILY GRAPHIC

FINIS CORONAT OPUS

ON BROOKLYN BRIDGE, NEW YORK SIDE.

PLATE 10

THE BROOKLYN BRIDGE

The longest suspension span in the world, the Brooklyn Bridge captured the imagination of people everywhere.

Though there are few visual identifiers in this watercolor, we may presume that we are looking at Manhattan, and that Sonntag's vantage point is the Brooklyn riverfront near to where the Manhattan Bridge would be built a few years later. To the right of the bridge we see a steamship, the scale of which may be assessed by the tugs alongside it. This in turn allows us to see the stupendous scale of the Brooklyn Bridge towering overhead.

The image conveys a sense of the raw power of the city. The Brooklyn Bridge was the longest suspension bridge that had ever been built, with a main span of 1,595 feet 6 inches, and at the time was the largest feat of steel construction in history.

While many artists wished to evoke the grace and beauty of the bridge, Sonntag chose to emphasize its awesome scale. The bridge dwarfs the steamship, soon to pass beneath the bridge en route to New York Harbor and, perhaps, a journey across the Atlantic Ocean.

PLATE 11

THE BOWERY AT NIGHT

By night the Bowery blazed, the El roaring overhead, hissing steam and throwing sparks.

When Sonntag painted this scene, the Bowery was a lively thoroughfare. Though not quite the working-class Broadway it had once been when Edwin Forrest trod the boards of the old Bowery Theatre, it was not yet the skid row the street would become in the twentieth century. Thronged nighttime sidewalks seem too full to fit another person.

The artist wonderfully captures New York's modes of transportation at a time of transition. Horse-drawn carriages pull up to the curb while early automobiles chug down the center of the road. By this time, electric trolleys had replaced the horsecars

of old, but the elevated railroad, seen at the left spewing its smoke into the night air, is still powered by steam.

The view is just to the north of Grand Street. At the far left the classical building, with a single fluted Corinthian column visible, is architect Stanford White's beautiful Bowery Savings Bank, which was completed in 1895. The bank still stands, now a fashionable restaurant in a trendy part of town. The dormered building to the right of the bank is also standing today.

PLATE 12

WASHINGTON ARCH, SPRING

This triumphal arch marks the beginning of the grand Fifth Avenue.

In 1889 New York celebrated the centennial of George Washington's swearing-in as the first president of the United States. As part of the festive decorations marking the event, architect Stanford White designed a temporary triumphal arch of lath and plaster, placed to tower over Fifth Avenue roughly in line with Washington Mews.

Greenwich Village residents liked the arch so much that they raised funds for White to create a permanent arch of marble from Westchester County. The permanent arch was placed a little to the south, within Washington Square. It was completed in 1892, one year before Hassam's painting, which shows the view south from Fifth Avenue through the arch into the square.

Today, one thing about the arch is notably different from what we see in this painting. In 1916 marble statues of George Washington—one showing him as general, the other as civilian—were placed before either pier, facing north onto the avenue.

PLATE 13

FIFTH AVENUE AT WASHINGTON SQUARE

Henry James wrote that this was one of the few neighborhoods of the city to have "something of a social history."

The elegantly attired lady, with billowy white skirt, closely fitted black coat, black bonnet, and orange parasol, attests to the persistence of gentility on Fifth Avenue just to the north of Washington Square as late as the 1890s.

These blocks first became fashionable in the 1830s, after the square had opened as a public park and elegant houses rose all around it. Henry James's novel *Washington Square*, published in 1881, is set here in the 1840s.

After the Civil War, most of the elite of Washington Square had moved uptown, to places like Murray Hill. However, pockets of old wealth clung tenaciously to the avenue that had, as Henry James wrote, "the look of having had something of a social history." Around this time, though, the neighborhood was changing. Artists had begun moving into old town houses renovated into studios, and the city was witnessing the beginnings of the massive immigration of southern Italians who would colonize the streets immediately south of Washington Square.

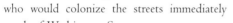

PLATE 14

LOWER FIFTH AVENUE

The brownstone churches north of Washington Square were perfect for the display of Sunday finery.

The artist's point of view is the east side of Fifth Avenue looking south toward the imposing Gothic tower of the First Presbyterian Church at Twelfth Street, built in 1846. Architect Joseph C. Wells based the church's tower on Magdalen Tower in the English university city of Oxford, dating from the late fifteenth century.

Just beyond, another set of Gothic finials etched against the sky belong to the Episcopal Church of the Ascension at Tenth Street. It was designed by Richard Upjohn and built in 1841, and is mentioned in Henry James's *Washington Square*.

In the lower left we see a couple descending the stoop of one of the brownstone mansions for which lower Fifth Avenue was famous. The churches themselves were faced in the brown sandstone that was widespread in New York by 1890. The men and women in their fine clothes crowding the sidewalk, and the elegant carriages in the street, suggest this is a Sunday, and that services have just concluded at these fashionable churches.

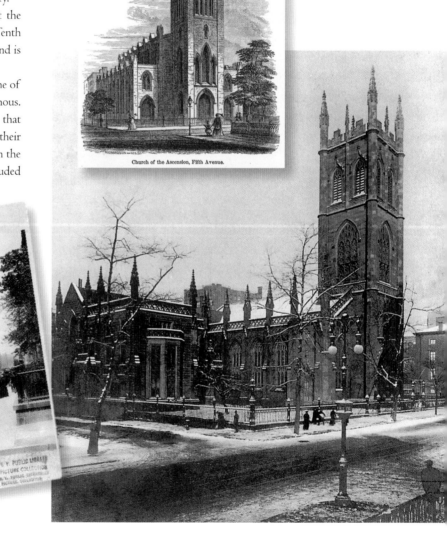

Church of the Ascension, Fifth Avenue.

FIFTH AVENUE ON SUNDAY.

N. Y. PUBLIC LIBRARY
PICTURE COLLECTION
N. Y. PUBLIC LIBRARY
PICTURE COLLECTION

PLATE 15

RAIN STORM, UNION SQUARE

New Yorkers stride purposefully across Union Square en route to dinner before the show.

The long dresses, the men's black frock coats, the black umbrellas, the carriages, and the rain-slicked pavements evoke a period when Union Square's days as an elegant residential outpost had already yielded to theaters, stores, and restaurants. We can see all the bustle and glamor of glowing commerce in the background.

Hassam noted that this scene takes place in late afternoon, and though he did not specify the day of the week, we can assume it is a workday. The well-dressed people likely did not live around there, so they may be leaving work, going shopping, or heading to dinner.

By the 1830s, when many of the city's elite families lived around the square, New York's development had already reached as far north as Union Square, at Fourteenth Street. As the city's rich, ever restless, moved farther north, high-end retailing moved in. Tiffany & Co. had its famous store on the west side of the square, while Brentano's Literary Emporium, New York's most famous bookstore, stood on the north side.

ON a damp day or a rainy day you need a rain-proof coat; on a clear cold day, a light-weight overcoat. Get a Watershed. It's truly an any-day coat. Stylish all the time — rain-proof when you need it.

You will always be in good company if you wear Kuppenheimer Clothes. Let our Guarantee Label be your guide. Go to the merchant in your city who advertises Kuppenheimer Clothes.

A booklet, Styles for Men, Volume 39, sent upon request.

PLATE 16

EARLY EVENING, UNION SQUARE

In 1902 Union Square was in transition, housing both the fashionable Tiffany & Co. and the offices of labor unions.

Hassam's lovely painting of spectrally elegant black-clad figures scurrying across a snow-covered square—perhaps anticipating boarding one of the oncoming carriages while the background blazes orange with the area's intense commerce and nightlife—was painted in a time of transition for Union Square.

Tiffany & Co. would remain on the west side of the square for only another four years before moving to Thirty-seventh Street. As opulent retail moved to midtown Fifth Avenue and the theaters moved to Times Square, labor unions, which were growing fast at the turn of the century, moved their headquarters into buildings around Union Square.

The name "Union Square" derives from the union, or intersection, of Broadway and Fourth Avenue, but the labor unions—for many years such an important element of the area—were more than happy to share the nickname.

Soon the streets around the square would emerge as the city's hub of discount or "bargain basement" retailing, a far cry from Tiffany. The figures and carriages in this painting, however, are a world away from the bargain basement.

THE NEW STORE OF MESSRS. TIFFANY & CO. UNION SQUARE, N. Y.—JOHN KELLUM, ARCHITECT.

IN FRONT OF TIFFANY'S UNION SQUARE

UNION SQUARE

PLATE 17

UNION SQUARE IN SPRING

A bronze Abraham Lincoln overlooks Dead Man's Curve, where cable-car accidents on the tight track were common.

Union Square is bordered by Fourteenth Street on the south, Fourth Avenue on the east, Seventeenth Street on the north, and Broadway on the west. The view here would appear to be from an upper floor on Seventeenth Street opposite the square, looking south. The wide avenue in the upper left is Fourth Avenue, and that in the upper right is Broadway.

The tall form just right of center, touching the top of the frame, is the spire of Grace Church, designed by James Renwick Jr. and built in 1846—the church that for many decades served the city's Episcopal elite. In the right center is the fountain installed in the square in 1842, when this was the city's most fashionable residential area. At Fourth Avenue and Fourteenth Street the intersecting roads formed the notorious Dead Man's Curve, where operators of cable cars such as those visible in the painting found it difficult to avoid collisions with other vehicles. The scene is vividly described in Caleb Carr's historical novel of New York, *The Alienist*, set in the very year this painting was made.

On an island in Dead Man's Curve stands Henry Kirke Brown's 1868 statue of Abraham Lincoln, whose funeral procession had paused here four years earlier for a prayer service.

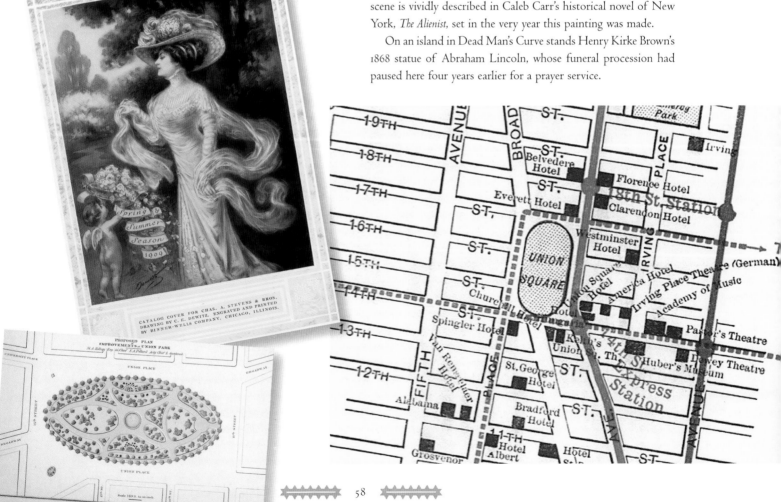

CATALOG COVER FOR CHAS. A. STEVENS & BROS. DRAWING BY C. H. DEWITZ. ENGRAVED AND PRINTED BY BINNER-WELLS COMPANY, CHICAGO, ILLINOIS.

PLATE 18

WINTER IN UNION SQUARE

Then, as now, Union Square was a light oasis in the otherwise cramped grid of Manhattan streets.

Hassam obviously loved Union Square, so often and so well did he paint it. Except perhaps for its earliest days when it was a fashionable residential area, Union Square has never been considered beautiful. In fact, through much of its history, particularly when Hassam was drawn to it, the square has had a haphazard and at times tawdry appearance.

Regardless, Hassam saw its virtue as a great well of light in the midst of the Manhattan grid. Here he could explore to his heart's content the dazzling effects of light on buildings and trees, and the always-rushing motion of pedestrians, carriages, and cable cars in different seasons, as in this wintry scene that in all likelihood he painted from a perch on an upper floor of the Century Building on Seventeenth Street between Broadway and Fourth Avenue.

This building, which is still standing, housed the *Century Magazine*, a quality monthly to which Hassam contributed illustrations. Beyond the cable cars slashing diagonally across the picture plane, and the trees that

laterally bisect the plane, rise the spire of Grace Church and the cast-iron domed Domestic Sewing Machine Building, designed in 1872 by Griffith Thomas, once New York's most prolific architect.

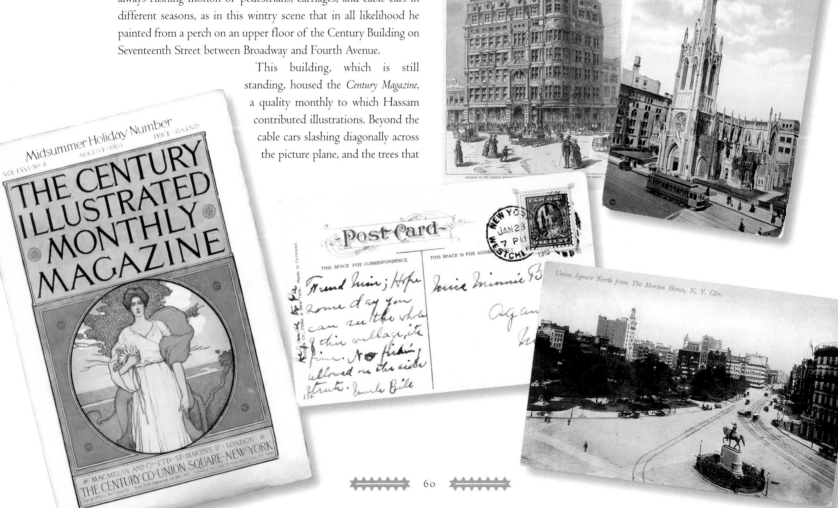

PLATE *19*

FIFTH AVENUE

By 1919 New York had entered overdrive; it had emerged from the First World War intact
while the capitals of Europe lay demoralized and bankrupt.

"Humanity in motion," Childe Hassam said, "is a continual study for me." New York had always been about humanity in motion. The British writer V. S. Pritchett once said that if Paris suggests intelligence, and London suggests experience, then New York suggests activity. This was probably never more true than in the years after the First World War, when the destruction of the morale and treasuries of the European capitals made New York the global capital of finance and business for the first time.

Hassam here captures the crowded avenue, now teeming with automobiles. The indistinctness of the buildings is no doubt intentional, since the artist wishes to suggest the mood of the city and not specific landmarks. However, it is possible that this is a view north from around Forty-seventh Street. If so, then at the top, just to the right of center, is the Scribner Building, designed by Ernest Flagg and built in 1913, while just to the right of the upper left corner is St. Patrick's Cathedral, its towers still rising higher than any other building in the picture.

Following the 1913 opening of the new Grand Central Terminal on Forty-second Street at Park Avenue, midtown was fast supplanting lower Manhattan as the city's central business district.

PLATE 20

FIFTH AVENUE IN WINTER

Brown sandstone, "like a cold chocolate sauce," coated New York in the second half of the nineteenth century.

This is Fifth Avenue as different as can be from Hassam's painting of 1919. New York was still the brownstone city, as we can see from the high-stooped Italianate houses in the upper left. In the street we see carriages and hansom cabs, and also the once popular horse-drawn omnibus, in red and black, of the Fifth Avenue Coach Company.

Motorized buses did not appear until 1905, and the horse-drawn buses were retired in that same year. In the lower half of the frame people walk under umbrellas through the falling snow, and a boy seems to be making a snowball.

This part of Fifth Avenue is evidently in transition from residential to mixed uses, and the date suggests it would be somewhere between Twenty-third and Forty-second streets. Edith Wharton wrote of "the brownstone of which the uniform hue coated New York like a cold chocolate sauce." The chocolate sauce is certainly cold in this picture.

PLATE 21

A SPRING MORNING

A beautiful May morning, and a carriage awaits the ladies of the family.

By the 1890s fashionable society had moved uptown from the Twentieth Street depicted by Hassam in this oil painting. Nonetheless, pockets of gentility persisted, as we see from the expensively attired ladies descending a brownstone stoop to enter a fancy carriage. This takes place in the shadow of Ladies' Mile, the fabled district of department stores that were at their peak of popularity and importance in New York at this time.

The golden dome belongs to Hugh O'Neill's store, an enormous department store known for its discounts and attraction to the general public, among whom the ladies in the foreground definitely do not belong. O'Neill's domes were later removed but were restored to the building in 2007.

The crenellated church tower visible in front of O'Neill's dome belongs to the Church of the Holy Communion, an 1840s Gothic Revival church in brownstone, designed by Richard Upjohn. A hundred years after Hassam painted this scene, the church had been converted into a discotheque.

PLATE 22

VIEW OF BROADWAY
AND FIFTH AVENUE

The lively space where these two main thoroughfares cross is filled with vehicles and pedestrians.

THE GRAND PARTY OF TO-DAY.

President Cleveland—"In this we bury all unkindness."

At the top of the painting we see a sign for the Victoria Hotel, on Fifth Avenue between Twenty-sixth and Twenty-seventh streets. At the time Hassam painted this scene, in 1890, President Grover Cleveland resided at the Victoria. This was between his two terms (1885–89 and 1893–97) as president.

In front of it stands the New York Club, at Twenty-fifth Street, spanning the distance between Fifth Avenue, the thoroughfare on the right, and Broadway on the left. Because it runs at a diagonal, roughly southeast to northwest, Broadway intersects most of the north–south avenues on the Manhattan grid. Broadway crosses Fifth Avenue at Twenty-third Street, a site now marked by the famous Flatiron Building, which would not be built for another twelve years.

We may presume that the flowered balcony in the foreground belongs to the Flatiron's predecessor on the site, the St. Germain Hotel. In 1890 this was a district of hotels and department stores. Indistinct though visible at the far left of the frame is the Fifth Avenue Hotel, which opened in the 1850s and was still the city's most renowned hostel in 1890.

A brownish obelisk is visible in the middle of the picture. This granite monument marks the burial place of General William Jenkins Worth, hero of the Mexican War of the 1840s. When the obelisk was erected in 1857, this was a quietly elegant residential section, and the monument was one of New York's notable civic adornments.

R. WALLACE & SONS MANUFACTURING CO., SILVERSMITHS.
No. 228 FIFTH AVENUE, BETWEEN 26TH AND 27TH STREETS, ADJOINING VICTORIA HOTEL.

PLATE 23

FLAT IRON BUILDING

"I found myself agape, admiring the prow of the Flatiron Building, ploughing up through the traffic of Broadway and Fifth Avenue in the late-afternoon light."

When Childe Hassam painted this intersection in 1890, as depicted in the previous painting, it was natural to show the view to the north. When the Flatiron (as it is more commonly spelled) Building opened in 1902, its compelling appearance made the southern view the one that interested visitors to the area. The author H. G. Wells, who wrote the epigraph above, was just one famous visitor to be appropriately impressed.

In the lower left we see the 1857 granite obelisk marking General William Jenkins Worth's burial place. The great thoroughfare shown in the left of the picture is Broadway.

The Flatiron Building, designed by D. H. Burnham & Co. of Chicago, is in the upper right of the painting. The building conforms to the triangular lot formed by Broadway's diagonal crossing of Fifth Avenue. Contrary to what many people think, the Flatiron was never the city's tallest building. But it must have seemed so, for it is completely freestanding, abutted by no other structure—a highly unusual thing in jam-packed New York.

The triangular form, freestanding quality, and beautifully patterned terra-cotta surfaces have made the building a favorite of New Yorkers, of painters like Colin Campbell Cooper, and especially of photographers such as Alfred Stieglitz and Edward Steichen.

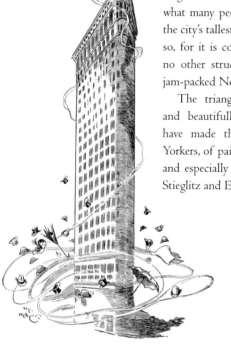

PLATE 24

THE METROPOLITAN TOWER

Sometimes called "New York's Campanile," the Met Life Tower is modeled on Venice's famous landmark.

This view south on Madison Avenue shows two of the city's principal landmarks from around 1910. The high tower on the left belongs to the second Madison Square Garden, designed by Stanford White of McKim, Mead & White, and built in the late 1880s on the block bordered by Madison Avenue, Twenty-sixth and Twenty-seventh streets, and Park Avenue South. Atop the main, low block of the structure was the roof garden where Harry K. Thaw infamously shot and killed White in 1906.

Madison Square Garden, with its large amphitheater and many exhibitions, conventions, and sporting events, was demolished in the 1920s. Its tower was modeled on the Giralda of the Cathedral in Seville, Spain.

The high tower on the right is that of the Metropolitan Life Insurance Company. When the fifty-story structure, designed by Napoleon Le Brun & Sons, was completed in 1909, it was the tallest office building in the world, a title it would hold until 1913. Its design was inspired by the campanile of San Marco in Venice. A few years earlier in 1902, the 400-year-old Venice bell tower had dramatically collapsed. New York's Metropolitan Life Insurance Company had taken a leading role in raising funds for the tower's restoration, and in the design of their own headquarters they may have wished to underscore their philanthropic reputation.

The tall, gray building in the center was the Twenty-fifth Street annex to the Metropolitan Life headquarters. Note the era's mix of automobile and horse-drawn vehicles on Madison Avenue.

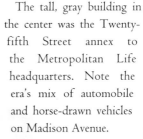

MADISON SQUARE GARDEN, N.Y. CITY.

PLATE 25

SPRING MORNING IN THE HEART OF THE CITY

"The true center of idle New York," wrote historian Mariana Griswold van Rensselaer of Madison Square.

In the 1890s Madison Square was still the heart of the city, attested to by the presence at the northwest corner of Fifth Avenue and Twenty-third Street of the Fifth Avenue Hotel, the portico of which is visible in the lower left of the painting. Built in the 1850s, the hotel stood for half a century as the city's most famous, boasting such guests as the Prince of Wales.

When Hassam reworked this painting in the late 1890s, however, the new Waldorf-Astoria at Fifth Avenue and Thirty-fourth Street had overtaken the Fifth Avenue

Hotel, which was demolished in the early twentieth century. The sidewalk clock to the right of the hotel's portico still stands, one of the few remaining of this lovely type of street furnishing.

On the right are the lawns and trees of Madison Square, bounded by Twenty-third Street, Madison Avenue, Twenty-sixth Street, and Fifth Avenue. Opened as a public park in the 1840s, it soon became the center of a fashionable residential area that then became a center of hotels, theaters, and department stores. Hassam's view does not take in Madison Square Garden, which stood from the 1880s to the 1920s across from the northeast corner of the square near the upper right of the painting.

PLATE 26

FIFTH AVENUE

For more than a century, the Waldorf-Astoria has been one of the world's most luxurious and innovative hotels.

The hotel that supplanted the Fifth Avenue Hotel as the city's most fashionable was the Waldorf-Astoria, which rose in two stages on the west side of Fifth Avenue between Thirty-third and Thirty-fourth streets in the 1890s. This tall, ornate structure dominates the left of the painting.

In the 1850s, when this part of Manhattan was emerging as a high-class residential district, the brothers John Jacob Astor III and William B. Astor built adjoining brownstone mansions. William Waldorf Astor, son of John Jacob III, envied the prestige accorded William B.'s wife, Caroline, who was known as Mrs. Astor, leader of New York society. A rather perturbable man, William Waldorf declared, upon losing a race for the United States Congress, that America was unfit for a gentleman, and therefore moved to England, where he eventually became Baron Astor of Hever Castle. His daughter-in-law, Nancy Langhorne, was the first British female Member of Parliament. When he left New York, he replaced his mansion with the Waldorf Hotel.

Soon thereafter, Caroline Astor and her son, John Jacob IV (who died on the *Titanic*), moved uptown and replaced their mansion with the Astoria Hotel. Though built separately, when the Astoria half was completed it operated as one with the Waldorf. Both halves were designed by Henry J. Hardenbergh, an architect favored by the Astor family.

The white-columned building just to the right of the hotel is Stanford White's Knickerbocker Trust Company, while the brownstone spire at Thirty-seventh Street belongs to Brick Presbyterian Church, built in the 1850s.

Waldorf-Astoria Hotel, New York City.

PLATE 27

THE MANHATTAN CLUB

An important institution that started life as the mansion of an Irish American entrepreneur-turned-multimillionaire.

This grand marble building, designed by John Kellum, was built in 1869. It was originally the mansion of Alexander T. Stewart, at the time the second richest man in New York after Cornelius Vanderbilt. Stewart's wealth came from dry goods retailing and wholesaling, and from real estate speculation. His store at Broadway and Tenth Street, opened in 1862, is considered by many historians to be the first full-fledged department store in the world.

From his humble Irish origins, Stewart worked his way up in the world—apparently the sin that made him an outcast in New York society. His choice of white marble for his home was provocative in an age when rich New Yorkers invariably chose dour brown sandstone. After Stewart's death, his house became a private club.

NEW YORK CITY.—RESIDENCE OF THE LATE ALEXANDER T. STEWART, CORNER OF THIRTY-FOURTH STREET AND FIFTH AVENUE.

Childe Hassam believed it to be so splendid that it "will stand as long as the city remains." He was wrong. The mansion was razed a few years later for the Knickerbocker Trust Company, designed by Stanford White, whose wife was, coincidentally, Stewart's niece. Stewart was buried in the churchyard of St. Mark's in the Bowery, whence his body was stolen and held for ransom. When the body was recovered, it was reinterred in a high-security mausoleum on Long Island.

AN ORIGINAL PHOTOGRAPH OWNED BY MERCHANTS' EXCHANGE NATIONAL BANK.
BROADWAY, WEST SIDE, FROM MURRAY TO WARREN STREET, IN 1863.
AT NO. 257, ON SITE AFTERWARDS AND STILL OCCUPIED BY MERCHANTS' EXCHANGE NATIONAL BANK, THE LATE ALEXANDER T. STEWART HAD HIS FIRST STORE.

ST. MARK'S CHURCH, Built in 1846

TENTH STREET AND 2ND AVENUE.

PLATE 28

THE EL

For more than half a century, New York's noisy elevated railways were a constant reminder of people on the move.

The indistinctness of the buildings makes it difficult to know which of Manhattan's Els Hassam has depicted here. A fair guess would be Sixth Avenue, judging from the fiery light emerging from the commercial establishments along the sidewalk, and the seemingly festive crowds of people. These indicate a place of spirited nightlife, and in 1894 the "Tenderloin" flourished in the shadow of the Sixth Avenue El. This was a place of bars, gambling dens, and other places of iniquitous behavior—and was world-famous.

The elevated railway, or El, was New York's first form of mass rapid transit, first operational in the 1870s. We see from the smoke emanating from the locomotives that these Els are still of the steam-powered variety. Soon they would run on electrical power, which eliminated the smoke. But electricity also meant that new trains could be built to run underground, thus making it possible to remove the ungainly elevated structures from the city's avenues.

The first subway began operation exactly ten years after Hassam painted this picture, though the Els would not be dismantled for another half century.

HERALD SQUARE, SIXTH AVENUE, BROADWAY AND THIRTY-FIFTH STREET

Elevated R. R. Curve at 110th Street, New York

PLATE 29

BROADWAY AND 42ND STREET

Snowy evening scenes were a great favorite of the New York Impressionists.

The diagonal of Broadway slashes across Seventh Avenue at Forty-second Street, forming a triangular island that was still known as Longacre Square when Hassam painted this picture in 1902; it would not be rechristened "Times Square" by a city council decree until two years later, when a station of the Interborough Rapid Transit subway opened beneath the new headquarters of the *New York Times*.

Well before the subway arrived, mass transit had made the area highly accessible. Elevated trains ran on Sixth and Ninth avenues, and, as we see in this picture, streetcars and carriages congested the roadways.

The area had been remote farmland when it was purchased in the early nineteenth century by New York's greatest real estate speculator, John Jacob Astor. By the end of the century,

development had reached all the way to the northern end of Manhattan island, and the theater district was moving northward from Herald Square to Longacre Square, which was also the center of carriage manufacturing and sales—and later of automobile sales.

The legendary Oscar Hammerstein built his Olympia Theatre at Broadway and Forty-fourth Street in 1895, and Times Square as we now know it began to take shape.

PLATE 30

TIMES SQUARE

Times Square, now an iconic world landmark and a symbol of its home city, is little more than a century old.

Times Square, New York City.

The tall, triangular tower clad in white terra-cotta that dominates the picture opened in 1904 as the headquarters of the *New York Times*, which had moved uptown from Newspaper Row near City Hall. The building stands on the triangular island where Broadway crosses Seventh Avenue at Forty-second Street.

The triangle was known as Longacre Square until 1904 when, concurrent with the construction of the Times Tower, a station of New York's first underground rapid transit train line, opened underneath the triangle. The Interborough Rapid Transit Company chose to name the station Times Square, and soon the city formally adopted the name.

At midnight on January 1, 1905, the *New York Times* sponsored a fireworks display to greet the New Year. Previously, New Yorkers had congregated at Broadway and Wall Street for the tolling of the bells of Trinity Church. Now the new Times Square became the world capital of New Year's Eve.

The famous ball drop, witnessed annually by hundreds of thousands of people packed into the streets to the north of the Times Tower—the viewpoint of Childe Hassam's painting—was inaugurated by the *New York Times* on January 1, 1907. Such drops were subsequently used in many other towns and cities to allow people to synchronize their clocks.

TIMES SQUARE, ELECTION NIGHT.

PLATE 31

HORSE-DRAWN CABS AT EVENING

As in cities the world over, the era of horse-drawn traffic was coming to an end.

The artist has positioned himself roughly at Fourth Avenue, now Park Avenue South, and Eighteenth Street, looking south toward Union Square, identifiable by the clump of trees in the upper left quadrant of the picture. The domed building behind the trees is the Domestic Sewing Machine Co. Building at Broadway and Fourteenth Street.

The main subject of Hassam's watercolor, however, is not Union Square but the horse-drawn cabs that were such an important fixture on New York streets at the time. They shared the streets with horse-drawn omnibuses, which were like the cabs except they were larger and carried more passengers, and horse-drawn street railways, which were similar to the omnibuses but glided on iron rails.

Horse-drawn urban transportation was supplemented by the steam-powered elevated trains. Soon, however, the streetcars and Els would be electrified, and with the automobile on the horizon, the days of the romantic cabs pictured here were numbered.

Hassam was fascinated by the effects of rain in the city. He loved viewing its streets through a veil of rain, both for what it did with the light pouring forth from restaurants and stores and for the way those lights reflected off rain-slicked sidewalks.

PLATE 32

NEW YORK PUBLIC LIBRARY

Lions named Patience and Fortitude, qualities claimed by New Yorkers over the decades, guard one of the world's great public libraries.

The artist is slightly elevated above Forty-second Street as he looks south on Fifth Avenue. Most of the right half of the picture is taken up by the monumental edifice of the New York Public Library, built in 1911 to the plans of architects John Merven Carrère and Thomas Hastings, and library director John Shaw Billings.

The library, which brought together several outstanding private collections, was one of New York's proudest achievements, and today ranks among the greatest libraries in the world, surpassed only by the national libraries of France, Britain, and the United States.

A dominating feature of the building is its generous Fifth Avenue terrace, which serves as a public plaza. In the painting we see the two lion statues that guard the steps leading to the terrace. During the Great Depression, New York's mayor, Fiorello LaGuardia, named the lions Patience and Fortitude, the qualities New Yorkers needed to cultivate to get through the bad times.

The mansard-roofed building at the southwest corner of Fifth Avenue and Fortieth Street was the headquarters and flagship retail store of the famous Knox Hat Company; the building was designed by John Duncan and built in 1902. To its right rises a twenty-story office building built in 1914, 6 West Fortieth Street, designed by Starrett and Van Vleck.

Announcing the Fall Style Book, the authority on men's styles; a special NEW YORK NUMBER

KNOX Fall Hats are now on sale at agencies in every important city in the world.

PLATE 33

OLD GRAND CENTRAL STATION

New York's principal railroad station was undergoing a major expansion at the beginning of the twentieth century.

When Colin Campbell Cooper painted this fascinating picture, Grand Central Station, as it was called at the time, was in the midst of its storied transformation into Grand Central Terminal. The original Grand Central Depot was built on Forty-second Street, straddling Park Avenue, in 1871. The facility for steam trains required vast open-air rail yards, which extended north from the depot on Park Avenue. The depot was enlarged in the 1890s, and architect Bradford Lee Gilbert changed its name from Grand Central Depot to Grand Central Station.

In Cooper's view south through the Park Avenue rail yards, we see the domed corner towers that Gilbert added to the station. This expansion was not enough, however, and when the railroads that the station served electrified their operations, thus making underground rail yards feasible, a whole new terminal rose between 1903 and 1913, during which all train operations had to carry on as normal. It was as part of this project that the Park Avenue yards were decked over and Park Avenue attained its exalted status. This is the moment in time captured by Cooper.

The year of this painting, 1906, was also the year Edith Wharton's best-selling novel, *The House of Mirth*, was published, with its memorable opening scene set in the Grand Central Station just as depicted by Cooper.

PLATE 34

THE CATHEDRAL AND FIFTH AVENUE

St. Patrick's majestic towers dominate Fifth Avenue, which was composed principally of the palatial dwellings of the rich.

St. Patrick's Cathedral rose on Fifth Avenue between Fiftieth and Fifty-first streets between 1858 and 1879. When it opened, it was not only the most imposing church in the city but the most imposing building of any kind.

It symbolized the growing presence of the Irish in New York. Around the time the cathedral was begun, roughly one out of three New Yorkers had been born in Ireland. Before the Irish arrived in large numbers, relatively few Catholics lived in New York. By 1879, however, the number of Catholics in the city clearly warranted a cathedral of such grandeur.

It attained even greater celebrity in 1888 upon completion of the twin towers—for years they were the tallest structures in New York. The masterpiece of architect James Renwick Jr., it deftly integrates English and French Gothic forms on a very constricted site, and is faced in white marble, a striking contrast to the prevailing brown of 1870s New York.

ST. PATRICK'S CATHEDRAL.

COBB DETROIT PHOTOGRAPHIC CO

6891 ST. PATRICK'S CATHEDRAL, NEW YORK

PLATE 35

CATHEDRAL SPIRES, SPRING MORNING

For many years, St. Patrick's Cathedral towered over midtown Manhattan like the cathedral of a medieval city.

At the turn of the twentieth century, Fifth Avenue in midtown was one of the most pleasant places in the city to promenade. Here the tidiest sidewalks in the city were lined still by the brownstone mansions of the Vanderbilts and other elite New York families.

Childe Hassam was fascinated with the intrusion upon this scene by the majestic St. Patrick's Cathedral, the fantastic twin towers of which were completed in 1888—and were therefore still relatively fresh at the time of this picture. In this, as in several other paintings, Hassam shows us how the cathedral towered over the surrounding city, every bit as much as a cathedral would in a medieval European town.

The cathedral's architect, James Renwick Jr., had an extremely narrow site to work with. In order to make his overall proportions work, he had to make the towers exceptionally high in relation to the square footage of their bases, with the result that the towers' dramatic, tapering ascent knows no equal from the Middle Ages.

Today, of course, while those towers continue to thrill, they no longer dominate the skyline; instead, St. Patrick's appears as one of the more modest structures in a part of town now filled with enormous skyscrapers.

St. Patrick's Cathedral.

PLATE 36

SUNDAY ON FIFTH AVENUE

Being seen in the right attire in the right place was an important part of the Sunday ritual.

In 1897 the New York historian and writer Mariana Griswold Van Rensselaer wrote, "On Sundays, after church-time, the sauntering was very general. If you knew anyone worth knowing in New York, you were pretty sure to find him on the avenue then."

The gentility of the Sunday promenade just oozes from this painting. The dominant figures would appear to be a mother and her daughter opulently attired in their finest clothes—the spectacle of fashion being perhaps as much a part of these people's devotion as the worship services they have recently attended. The meeting and greeting to which Van Rensselaer alluded is demonstrated by the frock-coated man to the left, tipping his top hat to a passerby.

While the elite residents of Fifth Avenue in this era were almost all Protestants, the towers that dominate the east side of the avenue belong to St.

Patrick's, the Roman Catholic cathedral at Fifty-first Street, meaning we may presume the mother and daughter stand near Fifty-fifth or Fifty-sixth streets. Farther on we see the old Temple Emanu-El, the great synagogue erected at Forty-third Street in the late 1860s and demolished in 1927.

JEWISH TEMPLE.
(Fifth avenue, corner Forty-third street.)

PLATE 37

SNOWSTORM, FIFTH AVENUE

The snow, which fell reliably every winter, covers the city in a romantic white mantle.

Yet again we see Childe Hassam's love of atmospheric effects, of viewing the city through a veil of rain or, in this case, snow. New York is not now a notably snowy city, but winters were once colder, and it snowed much more regularly than today.

Here we see Fifth Avenue. It is difficult to discern exactly where, though clearly it is a residential section, as the houses are the bay-windowed brownstones in which New York abounded at the time, and still does in some parts of the city. On the left we see a man pushing a cart—perhaps a vendor of the roasted chestnuts that were once so popular during winter in New York. On the right we see a lady with an umbrella, and in the front a young boy appears to be making a snowball.

Around the time of this painting, architects and people of fashion had rebelled against the brownstone city. They balked that a city with New York's Roman skies should use light-colored materials. Even they, however, would have had to agree that the city's brownstones look achingly beautiful when they are draped and outlined in fresh, white snow.

PLATE 38

LATE AFTERNOON, NEW YORK

The fascination of a city in the grip of a snowstorm lures Hassam from the comfort of his studio.

William H. Gerdts, the foremost authority on American Impressionist painting, has written, "Hassam's fascination with the city seen in the rain or during a snowstorm sometimes makes it difficult to identify an actual location, as in his *Late Afternoon, New York*." Indeed, this is a difficult location to pin down. It appears to be midtown Manhattan, only because the combination of brownstone row houses and tall commercial or apartment buildings was at this time a feature of that part of the city. The street is wide, indicating that it is an avenue or a major cross-street such as Fifty-seventh Street.

OSBORNE FLATS, 57TH STREET AND 7TH AVENUE

We know that Hassam kept a studio on Fifty-seventh Street, so it is not too much to suggest that this is a view of it west toward Seventh Avenue, where the indistinctly rendered tall building on the north (right) side of the street is the Osborne, a luxury apartment building, that was completed at the northwest corner of Fifty-seventh Street and Seventh Avenue in the 1880s, and still stands today.

Here the city is seen through a blizzard, the wind-driven snow falling at a slant from north to south, no doubt making it very difficult for the horses to pull their carriages along a street of fast-accumulating snow. Again, the dark-hued buildings with their electrically lighted rooms create for Hassam a subject of the greatest visual fascination.

FALL & WINTER .1909 ~ 1910

The B Type of Coat

Simple, Serviceable, Beautifully Tailored

HARPER'S 1897

THE JANUARY NUMBER CONTAINS
White Man's Africa, by POULTNEY BIGELOW.
—The Martian, by DU MAURIER.—Farce, by
W. D. HOWELLS.—Short Stories, by Miss WIL-
KINS, BRANDER MATTHEWS, and E. A. ALEX-
ANDER.—Science at the Beginning of the
Century, Illustrated.—Literary Landmarks
of Rome, by LAURENCE HUTTON, etc., etc.

PLATE 39

COLUMBUS CIRCLE

One of the city's major intersections, Columbus Circle combines classical proportions and unplanned urban jumble.

Of all Broadway's intersections, the crossing at Eighth Avenue offers the greatest opportunity for urban grandeur. Here, rather than the customary X formed by such crossings, there is a traffic circle, in the center of which stands a magnificent monument, a rostral column surmounted by a Carrara marble statue of Christopher Columbus, created by Gaetano Russo, a Sicilian sculptor. The monument was dedicated seventeen years before Colin Campbell Cooper's painting.

As in 1909, when this picture was painted, the circle has ever been a motley assortment of buildings of mixed heights, sizes, and colors. Yet it is precisely that mixed quality that appeals to the painter, who here masterfully renders the vibrant jumble of it all.

On the left, the structure with the high domed tower is the Majestic Theatre, which opened in 1902 and which was owned by newspaper baron William Randolph Hearst, the model for Charles Foster Kane in Orson Welles's classic 1941 film, *Citizen Kane*. In the top center, the Church of the Paulist Fathers (1876–85), the city's second largest Roman Catholic church, rises majestically a cross-town block away at Ninth Avenue.

Our view is to the west, away from Central Park, which begins just outside the frame in the lower right, toward the blue water of the Hudson River.

PLATE 40

NIGHTFALL OVER COLUMBUS CIRCLE

A well-known painting whose accepted title belies its true subject,
one of the most intimate nighttime scenes from this romantic period.

This watercolor by Louis Sonntag Jr. is everywhere identified by the title *Nightfall Over Columbus Circle*, which is very odd, because it is patently not Columbus Circle. This is a view north from the crossing of Fifth Avenue and Broadway at Twenty-third Street.

The picture shows several interesting things. In the foreground is one of the improbably elaborate, though very lovely, electroliers that once lighted some Manhattan thoroughfares. Electricity, still somewhat novel at the time, is a theme here, for on the left we see an electric streetcar, or trolley, as such conveyances were known. Beyond the electrolier we see, without much detail, the granite obelisk erected in 1857 to mark the burial place of General William Jenkins Worth.

At that time, this was a genteel, quiet residential neighborhood. By the time of Sonntag's painting, it had become the bustling heart of the city. The trees visible to the right of the obelisk belong to Madison Square, bounded by Twenty-third and Twenty-sixth streets, and Fifth and Madison avenues. The thoroughfare receding into the distance to the left of the obelisk is Broadway; to the right is Fifth Avenue.

Depictions of dusk and dampness were hallmarks of Sonntag's work.

PLATE 41

CHURCH OF THE PAULIST FATHERS

The Paulist Fathers were founded in 1858 to further a practical
urban mission, and their church celebrates the solidity of their purpose.

Childe Hassam might have labeled this painting by the names of any of the three buildings that equally dominate the view. In the foreground, the castellated structure is the First Battery National Guard Armory, built in 1901. Located on Sixty-sixth Street between Central Park West and Columbus Avenue, the armory now serves as studios for the American Broadcasting Company.

At the time this painting was made, Hassam kept a studio on the corresponding block of Sixty-seventh Street, which we may presume is the vantage point from which the scene was rendered. The high-domed structure is the Empire Hotel on Broadway between Sixty-third and Sixty-fourth streets. A different building of the same name now stands on the site.

The church for which the painting is named dominates the background. When the Church of the Paulist Fathers was built between 1876 and 1885, it was the second-largest Roman Catholic church in New York City after St. Patrick's Cathedral on Fifth Avenue. It is located at Columbus Avenue between Fifty-ninth and Sixtieth streets. We are looking directly toward where the Lincoln Center for the Performing Arts would rise in the 1960s.

PLATE 42

ACROSS THE PARK

Hassam possibly painted this tranquil scene to take his mind off the constant noise of construction work.

In 1912 an anonymous *New York Times* art critic wrote that this springtime scene "interprets in purity of tone and lovely aspiring lines the sweet stimulating quality of the season."

The view is from the southwest, presumably from Hassam's Sixty-seventh Street studio, with Central Park's sheepfold in the foreground. The street in the bottom of the frame is Central Park West. It had been only thirty to forty years since the park, designed by Calvert Vaux and Frederick Law Olmsted, was more or less completed. At that time, around 1870, few if any of the buildings across the park on the Upper East Side would have been visible.

With the dramatic growth of the city in the late nineteenth century, the park was a pastoral haven for New Yorkers—such as these riding horseback for leisure on a fine spring day. In 1904, when Hassam painted this picture, the Upper West Side was in a state of agitated transformation as large apartment houses—the largest in the world—went up one after another following the opening of the city's first subway line, which extended up Broadway from Forty-second Street. There is no doubt that Hassam's contemplative scene was painted amid the nerve-jangling noise of heavy construction activity.

PLATE 43

CENTRAL PARK

Conservatory Water is still a favorite place for Upper East Side residents to walk their babies and toddlers.

This time Childe Hassam shows us the eastern side of the park. The body of water is known as the Conservatory Water.

Calvert Vaux and Frederick Law Olmsted had planned a greenhouse for this site, between Seventy-third and Seventy-fifth streets just west of Fifth Avenue. Instead, a small pond surrounded by beautiful plantings took shape. Since it adjoined the Upper East Side, which in its turn was taking shape as the most affluent residential district of the city, the Conservatory Water became a favored spot for rich mothers—or their hired nannies—and children to take afternoon strolls. It is remarkable how often this small part of the park, uncharacteristic as it is of Vaux and Olmsted's overall design, captured the attention of painters of the period, as in both this painting and the next, by William Merritt Chase.

The greenhouse was instead built at 105th Street, just west of Fifth Avenue. It was dismantled in the 1930s and its land transformed into the elegant Conservatory Garden. Thus, while the name "conservatory" abounds in Central Park, there is in fact no conservatory.

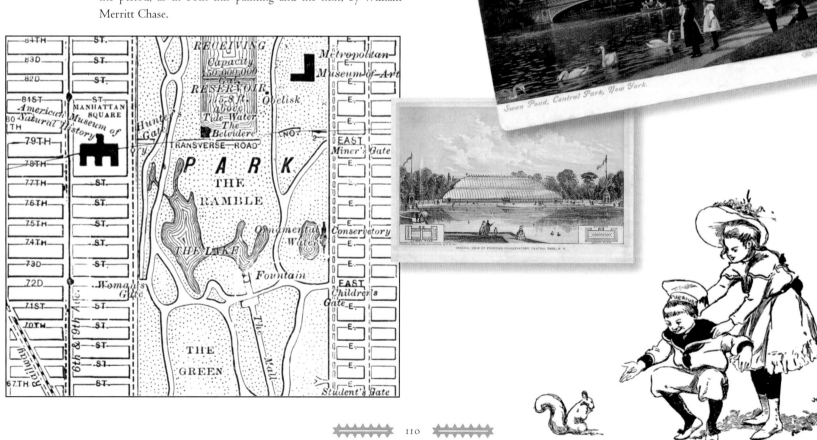

Swan Pond, Central Park, New York.

GENERAL VIEW OF PROPOSED CONSERVATORY, CENTRAL PARK, N.Y.

PLATE 44

LAKE FOR MINIATURE YACHTS

Sailing model yachts was considered an eminently safe and practical way for boys to expend energy.

Painted around the same time as the preceding image by Childe Hassam, William Merritt Chase here shows us the Conservatory Water in one of its typical uses, as a place for the sailing of model boats. For many years upper-class New York children sailed and raced model yachts on this body of water. The scene was immortalized in the 1945 children's book *Stuart Little* by E. B. White, from which the popular 1999 film was adapted.

The view here is to the west. In the far distance the tops of Central Park West buildings peek above the trees. The gabled structure at the top center is probably the famous Dakota Apartments, completed in 1884. In the upper right we can just make out the park's boathouse and lake. The area of the park in the top left is known as Pilgrim Hill.

The area of the Conservatory Water is a hollow that was part of the original topography of the park site. The city acquired most of the land for the park in 1853. The parcel was then systematically denuded of most of its unprepossessing topography. The area of the Conservatory Water belongs to a marshy terrain that once extended all the way across the park site from west to east.

Model Yachts on Lake, Central Park, New York.

PLATE 45

CENTRAL PARK

A snowy evening setting highlights the contrast between the icy park and the warm urbanity beyond.

Here we are looking west across the park. At the top are several well-known West Side structures. Near the left edge of the frame we can just make out the columned portico of the Congregation Shearith Israel Synagogue (1897) on Central Park West at Seventieth Street. To its right, at Seventy-second Street, rises the Hotel Majestic (1894) which, because it was replaced in 1931 by the present Majestic apartment building, tells us that Colin Campbell Cooper's undated picture must have been painted before that date.

The very tall building to the right of the Hotel Majestic is an apartment building called the Oliver Cromwell, built in 1927 on Seventy-second Street between Central Park West and Columbus Avenue. It was designed by Emery Roth. This is another clue that the picture was made before 1930, for otherwise another Emery Roth–designed building, the San Remo Apartments on Central Park West at Seventy-fourth Street, would be clearly visible to the right of the Oliver Cromwell.

The view is from the pond in the southeastern corner of the park. Crossing the pond is the Gapstow Bridge, built in 1896, and between the bridge and Central Park West lies Sheep Meadow.

PLATE 46

A BIT OF THE TERRACE

A sunny pastoral shows this popular part of Central Park inhabited
exclusively by wealthy mothers and their servants.

Apart from the way the people are dressed, this scene is identical today to the way it appeared around 1890, when it was painted by William Merritt Chase.

This is the northwesternmost part of the Terrace, on the line of Sixth Avenue between Seventy-second and Seventy-third streets. Because we see only its corner, we do not see what a grand structure the Terrace is. It culminates in the Mall, the only straight-line alley in the park, running at a southeast-to-northwest diagonal from Sixty-sixth to Seventy-second streets. The Terrace features a large patio at the edge of the lake—again, because we see but part of it, we cannot tell that the lake is of a substantial size.

The wooded area dominating the top half of the picture is the part of the park called Cherry Hill, which featured a carriage turnaround with a fountain for thirsty horses. This picture was probably painted on a sunny weekday afternoon, when the only people enjoying the park were mothers, nannies, and young children. Calvert Vaux and Frederick Law Olmsted intended that the park should serve equally the needs of New Yorkers of all social classes, yet in this picture the park looks rather like an exclusive upper-class resort.

Terraces in Central Park, New-York.

Bethesda Fountain, Central Park, New York.

PLATE 47

TERRACE AT THE MALL, CENTRAL PARK

Overlooking the lake, Bethesda Terrace is one of the most popular parts of Central Park, and a common meeting place.

William Merritt Chase painted this picture of the Terrace around the same time that he painted the preceding one. Again it is a weekday scene, as only well-dressed, parasol-wielding women are visible. On the weekend, the Terrace would be crowded on a fine day such as this.

The great sandstone Terrace is the heart of Central Park. The view is to the west. The grand stairs that descend from the Mall belong to a structure designed by the Englishman Jacob Wrey Mould, who should be counted—with Calvert Vaux, another Englishman, and Frederick Law Olmsted—as one of the principal architects of Central Park. Mould had worked in London for the famous British designer Owen Jones. Together, Jones and Mould worked on the decoration and internal arrangements of Sir Joseph Paxton's Crystal Palace at the Hyde Park exhibition of 1851. Mould, like

Jones, was an authority on Moorish architecture, from which he drew in his design of the Terrace, with its feeling of the Alhambra in Granada.

Chase's impressionistic brushwork fails to show the intricate stone carving with which the Terrace is lavished, making it a structure that can be studied and enjoyed for hours at a time. Just out of the frame to the right, we also do not see the famous bronze statue of the *Angel of the Waters*, by Emma Stebbins, in the center of the broad patio.

Bethesda Fountain and Terrace. Central Park.

The Terraces, Central Park, New York.

PLATE 48

SUMMER IN THE PARK

The role of women in the wealthier stratum of New York society was in flux,
and many had yet still to experience any sense of true freedom.

This haunting image of a finely dressed woman strolling in the sunshine in the verdant setting of what we presume to be Central Park calls to mind Edith Wharton's heroine Lily Bart in *The House of Mirth*, which takes place around the time Childe Hassam painted scenes like this.

Such a woman in New York society would have led a life rich in companions and activities. She would have been educated not in schools but at home by tutors and governesses. She would have learned languages, how to write and speak proper English, how to dance a dozen socially necessary dances, how to ride, and how to present herself ornamentally in the company of her peers. Her brothers, meanwhile, would have gone to Harvard or Columbia.

But if such a woman had an independent streak, a desire to step out from prescribed roles, as Edith Wharton did, then she might—as we sense may be the case with the woman

Hassam has painted—feel entirely alone in the world. What is haunting—and reminiscent of the tragic destiny of Lily Bart—is that this lone woman strides toward us out of the sunshine and into the shadow.

PLATE 49

THE COMMON, CENTRAL PARK

A wonderful expanse of green, a tribute both to the artistic freedom of
American Impressionism and to the vastness of New York's largest park.

This remarkable view is south across the Sheep Meadow in the southwestern part of Central Park. The meadow is eerily empty.

In the distance is one of the great early apartment-house complexes of New York, known as the Navarro, or the Spanish Flats, on Fifty-ninth Street (Central Park South) between Sixth and Seventh avenues. The gigantic complex comprised eight thirteen-story buildings; the Spanish developer, Jose Francisco de Navarro, named them the Madrid, the Cordova, the Granada, the Valencia, the Lisbon, the Barcelona, the Saragossa, and the Tolosa. They were designed by Hubert and Pirsson, architects of the famous Chelsea Hotel on West Twenty-third Street, and built in stages throughout the 1880s.

Rich New Yorkers had only recently begun living in multiple dwellings, which had previously been considered suitable only for the poor. Navarro, in building a complex more than twice the size of the 1884 Dakota on Seventy-second Street at Central Park West, overestimated the market, and the Spanish Flats not only failed to make money but caused the apartment-house bubble to burst—at least for a while.

By the end of the century, Manhattan had run out of land, and simple economics dictated that no matter how rich you were, you were very likely to live in an apartment building. The Navarro, spectacular as it was, lasted only until the 1920s, when it yielded to such new buildings as the New York Athletic Club and the Essex House Hotel.

PLATE 50

THE HOVEL AND THE SKYSCRAPER

Above all, the New York of a hundred years ago was a city of almost unimaginable contrasts.

The title of Childe Hassam's painting may, to the modern observer, symbolize a social-realist contrast of rich and poor, but that appears to be far from what the painter actually had in mind. Rather, as the art historian William H. Gerdts has written, Hassam, like many other artists of his time, delighted in depictions of the new city rising against the backdrop of the old.

The "hovel" refers not to derelict living quarters but to the Sixty-seventh Street stables on the west side of Central Park. With their snow-covered roofs, they can be seen right in the middle of the picture, which is a view east across Central Park—in all probability another view from Hassam's studio on West Sixty-seventh Street. The skyscraper, meanwhile, is what we see rising up from the bottom of the frame, the steel structure climbing up the left side of the picture.

Note the marvelous details, like the horseback riders just to the left of the stables. All the time Hassam had his Sixty-seventh Street studio, one of the fastest-developing neighborhoods in America, and the sounds of progress, rang daily in the painter's ears. The year of this picture, 1904, brought scads of development to the Upper West Side in the wake of the opening of the Interborough Rapid Transit subway line—the city's first—along Broadway.

PLATE 51

SPRINGTIME, WEST 78TH STREET

These comfortable middle-class west-side blocks were the epitome of modernity a hundred years ago.

This is a view west on Seventy-eighth Street toward the Hudson River. Beyond it is New Jersey, visible as a horizontal lavender band three-quarters of the way up the picture.

This is a fine Manhattan neighborhood scene, not far in place or time from the apartment-house setting of Theodore Dreiser's 1900 novel *Sister Carrie*. Though the scene looks old-fashioned to us today, this was one of the most modern places in America at the time. The homes in this quarter boasted electricity, telephones, indoor plumbing, central heating, elevators, and dumbwaiters, and were affordable to a burgeoning, if still insecure, middle class of small-business owners and corporate managers.

In *Sister Carrie*, Hurstwood, Carrie's husband, owns, then loses, a downtown restaurant. He and Carrie are portrayed passing through this neighborhood on their way down, during which time they meet the Vances, who are passing through on their way up.

The land slopes downward to the river. At this time Riverside Park, which is cut off from the perspective, did not extend all the way to the riverfront. The park was extended in the 1930s. Rather, the tracks of the New York Central Railroad, now encased in a tunnel, roared in the open air along the eastern bank of the Hudson.

PLATE 52

WOMAN ON A DOCK, ROTTEN ROW, BROOKLYN

Viewing the rotting hulks of wooden warships was a favorite riverside activity for the residents of Brooklyn.

When William Merritt Chase painted this scene, a Brooklyn Navy Yard pier called "Rotten Row" was open as a public promenade where New Yorkers went to view old warships.

The Brooklyn Navy Yard was founded in 1801 by the United States Navy as a major shipyard for the construction and repair of naval ships. Throughout much of its history, it was the most important facility of its kind in America, and remained in operation until 1966. For much of its history, it was strictly off-limits to the general public—as it is again today, having been converted into a large industrial park.

In 1886, when this picture was painted, the United States was not at war. The last major naval engagements had been in the American Civil War more than twenty years earlier, and the Spanish-American War was still some years away. The Navy had little to do but to put its surplus of ships on display, and Rotten Row obviously attracted some very well-heeled visitors, as we can see from the finely-dressed lady.

NAVY YARD, BROOKLYN, N. Y.

Receiving Ship Vermont, Brooklyn Navy Yard.

PLATE 53

IN BROOKLYN NAVY YARD

A quiet backwater amid the heavy industrialization of the East River shoreline.

The viewer would never guess this was a scene from within one of America's most important military installations, but in these quiet times for the United States, parts of the Brooklyn Navy Yard were open to the public.

The previous picture showed Rotten Row, a pier for the viewing of aged warships. In this image, however, we see a far less gritty, and more parklike, scene. The Navy Yard in 1887 was situated along a Brooklyn waterfront that was heavily industrialized. Shipyards, sugar refineries, ironworks, glassworks, oil refineries, printing houses, musical instrument manufacturers, machine works, cardboard box makers, coffee and tobacco warehouses, and much more crammed the waterfronts of the industrial city.

The harbor and the rivers were the economic lifeblood of New York, and public recreational access to waterfronts was much rarer than today. So when parts of the Brooklyn Navy Yard were opened, the novelty of the setting proved popular to the affluent classes from nearby inland Brooklyn communities such as Clinton Hill and Fort Greene—so near, yet also so far from the water.

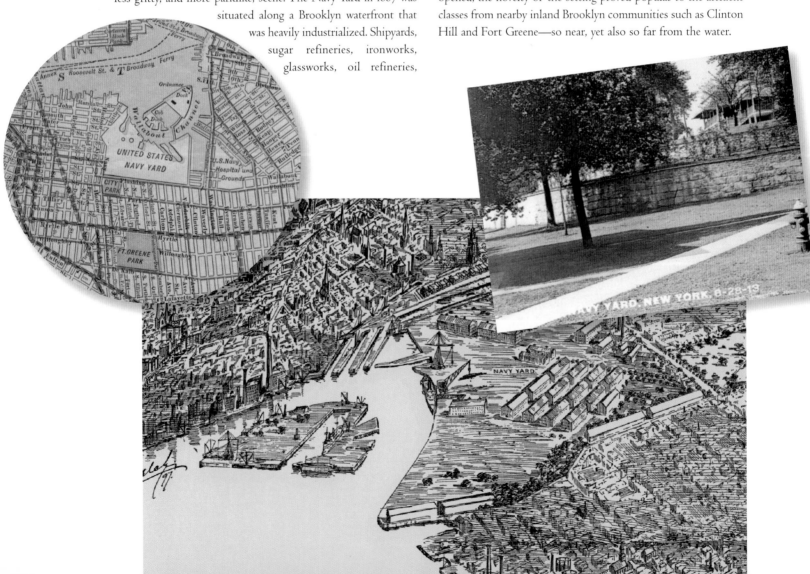

PLATE 54

HARBOR SCENE, BROOKLYN DOCKS

The docks and buildings of the Navy Yard are relegated to the far distance,
the expanse of water reminding the viewer of Brooklyn's riverside origins.

Similar to much of Brooklyn's waterfront, with the many vertical accents of ships' masts and factory smokestacks, this is Wallabout Bay, with a view to the Brooklyn Navy Yard that we saw in the two previous pictures by Chase.

To the left are the verdant grounds that we saw more intimately in those two images. Here the artist widens his angle of vision to show us the larger context. The ships we see are the docked warships of Rotten Row, but fully three-quarters of the picture is taken up by the silvery blue water of the bay, a fine reminder of New York's watery essence.

In this bay, thousands of American soldiers died in appalling conditions on British prison ships during the American Revolution. Later, in 1801, less than twenty years after the cessation of hostilities with Great Britain, the United States Navy established its most important shipbuilding and ship-repair facility here—just in time to build new warships for the War of 1812 against Great Britain.

PLATE 55

THE EAST RIVER

A lone oarsman passes a couple of East River dredgers in a watery world.

Here is another view from almost exactly the same place as the previous painting. The water and the sky, which together consume most of the picture's surface, appear as one, with the city a horizontally attenuated reddish-brown belt punctuated by smokestacks and the spindly masts of wooden ships.

At the time Chase painted this scene, Brooklyn was an independent city. New York City comprised Manhattan and part of lower Westchester County, the southern part of the present Bronx borough, while Brooklyn, a city on the western end of Long Island, had only recently been physically joined to Manhattan by the Brooklyn Bridge, completed in 1883.

Brooklyn was a major city, at this time the fourth largest in the United States. During the American Civil War it had been third; later, the phenomenal growth of Chicago pushed it down a place. Chicago was growing at such a rate that experts predicted that after the turn of the twentieth century it would replace New York as the nation's largest city. In 1898 the cities of New York and Brooklyn merged, forming a city so much larger than Chicago that it would never catch up.

PLATE 56

BOAT HOUSE, PROSPECT PARK

"Messing about in boats" was a favorite leisure pastime, especially for young couples looking for a little privacy.

This is a view south across the Lullwater, an appendage of the lake in the southeastern part of Brooklyn's Prospect Park. The rustic boathouse was replaced by a fine Beaux Arts classical structure in 1904, only a few years after this picture was painted.

The 585-acre Prospect Park was built in the years after the Civil War when Brooklyn, which was then an independent city, felt it had to have a great metropolitan greensward to compete with Central Park in New York City. Brooklyn hired Calvert Vaux and Frederick Law Olmsted, who had designed Central Park, but gave them much more political support and creative freedom than New York City had, with the result that both designers, as well as most critics, agreed that Prospect Park was a far greater work of art than Central Park.

For a number of years, William Merritt Chase resided in Brooklyn, and his Prospect Park pictures bring out a quality that Central Park lost early on, one which Prospect Park retains to this day. Because the neighborhoods that grew up around the Brooklyn park were low-rise districts of row houses, Prospect Park affords a feeling of remoteness from the city that Vaux and Olmsted had originally hoped that Central Park would provide.

PLATE 57

PROSPECT PARK, BROOKLYN

The grounds of this beautifully maintained garden were a popular place
to promenade, to find a spot to rest, or to seek inspiration.

In the southeastern part of Prospect Park is the Concert Grove, only a few steps away from the boathouse of the previous picture. It may be said of the Concert Grove that it is Prospect Park's most formal element, in the way Bethesda Terrace is the most formal part of Central Park. Like Bethesda Terrace, the design of the Concert Grove, by Calvert Vaux, is romantic, with intricately carved New Brunswick sandstone. As the name implies, this part of the park was intended for music.

We see a well-dressed woman at the top of steps that led to groves of trees along formal pathways adorned with bronze sculptures. On either side were concourses where carriages could congregate for concerts. The Concert Grove is right on the shore of the Lake, and musicians performed from a small island just offshore, while canopied seating along the shore lay between the musicians and the wooded groves.

At the far right of the picture is the Calvert Vaux-designed octagonal open-air structure that was called the Oriental Pavilion, for the Hindu influences evident in its design. New York's Impressionists, Childe Hassam and William Merritt Chase, were fascinated by finely dressed women all alone in parks or on city streets.

PLATE 58

A CITY PARK

Brooklyn's Tompkins Park was a welcome oasis for the leisured ladies of the neighborhood.

Here is another image of feminine solitude by William Merritt Chase. This is a small park named Tompkins Park, now called Herbert von King Park. It was laid out in the 1870s by Calvert Vaux and Frederick Law Olmsted as a simple, one-square-block residential park in what was the prosperous neighborhood of Bedford-Stuyvesant during late nineteenth-century Brooklyn.

The area, which is now undergoing a renaissance, suffered in the second half of the twentieth century from poverty and physical decline. When Chase painted this picture, he lived on Marcy Avenue, one of the streets bordering the park. It was a quiet, bourgeois neighborhood of tidy lawns, handsomely attired ladies with parasols, and frolicking children.

The park was originally named for New York governor and two-term U.S. vice president Daniel D. Tompkins, who was also an abolitionist. The simple design shows that Vaux and Olmsted believed the purposes of large metropolitan parks such as Prospect Park differed greatly from small neighborhood parks, which were mainly for taking a little air, letting the children run around, and listening to music, and required simple borders of flowers, lawns, and gravel paths, with none of the elaborate landscape features of the larger parks.

PLATE 59

TOMPKINS PARK

An urbane park in an urban setting, the neat lawns and flower beds mirror the daily lives of Brooklyn's wealthier inhabitants.

The sun-dappled paths of Bedford-Stuyvesant's Tompkins Park—with its manicured lawns and flower beds, church steeples rising in the distance above the trees, and mothers dressed in white with bonnets and parasols—gives us a vivid sense of Brooklyn in the late nineteenth century.

Today's Brooklyn borough was originally six towns, established under the Dutch in the seventeenth century. One of the towns, called Brooklyn, became an independent city in 1834. Between 1855 and 1896, the other five towns joined the City of Brooklyn, before Brooklyn itself merged with New York City in 1898.

Bedford-Stuyvesant lay within the original town of Brooklyn, which throughout the nineteenth century was dominated by genteel families of New England lineage. By the 1880s, when this picture was painted, many of the residents of Bedford-Stuyvesant had moved to the neighborhood's stately brownstone row houses from older parts of Brooklyn, such as Brooklyn Heights, and brought with them the quiet manners and high-mindedness that were their New England inheritance.

PLATE 60

WASH DAY, BROOKLYN

A hundred years ago, laundry drying in backyards on a Monday morning was a pervasive sight in every city.

In contrast to the images of Tompkins Park, we see here the intimate setting of William Merritt Chase's own Marcy Avenue backyard in Bedford-Stuyvesant.

Brooklyn, unlike Manhattan, was and remains a place of private houses, which in the late nineteenth century underwent a transformation from a place of private houses to a city of apartment buildings. Bedford-Stuyvesant is one of Brooklyn's classic brownstone neighborhoods. The houses all have rear yards where, as in this picture, the laundry was hung out to dry.

The house, strictly speaking, was that of Chase's wife's parents. Chase had married Alice Gerson, one of his models, in 1886, and for a time the newlyweds resided in her parents' home. The yard is not very deep. The typical row house stood on a hundred-foot-deep lot, so the backyard was at most thirty feet deep.

Note the wooden fence to the posts of which the clotheslines are connected. This marks the end of one backyard and the beginning of another. Because of all the contiguous backyards, the many mature trees, and the modest scale and earthen tones of the houses, much of Brooklyn, especially when viewed from above, looks like one giant park. We can see why any artist would have been transfixed by this simple scene with its play of sunshine and shadow and the perspective effects of the converging clotheslines.

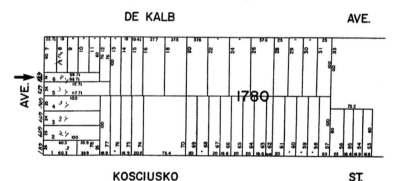

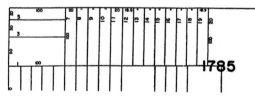

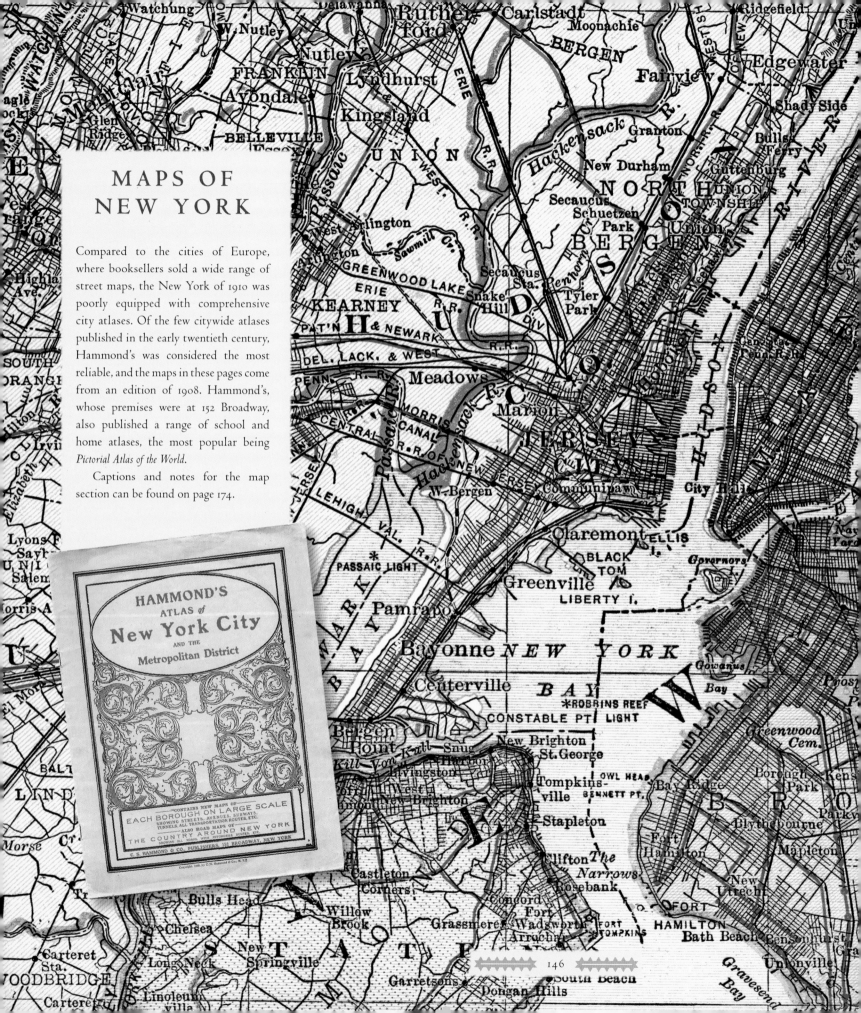

MAPS OF
NEW YORK

Compared to the cities of Europe, where booksellers sold a wide range of street maps, the New York of 1910 was poorly equipped with comprehensive city atlases. Of the few citywide atlases published in the early twentieth century, Hammond's was considered the most reliable, and the maps in these pages come from an edition of 1908. Hammond's, whose premises were at 152 Broadway, also published a range of school and home atlases, the most popular being *Pictorial Atlas of the World*.

Captions and notes for the map section can be found on page 174.

HAMMOND'S
ATLAS of
New York City
AND THE
Metropolitan District

CONTAINS NEW MAPS OF
EACH BOROUGH ON LARGE SCALE
SHOWING STREETS, AVENUES, SUBWAY,
TUNNELS, ALL TRANSPORTATION ROUTES, ETC.
ALSO ROAD MAPS OF
THE COUNTRY AROUND NEW YORK
SHOWING ALL ROADS, WITH AUTOMOBILE ROUTES, ETC.

C. S. HAMMOND & CO., PUBLISHERS, 152 BROADWAY, NEW YORK

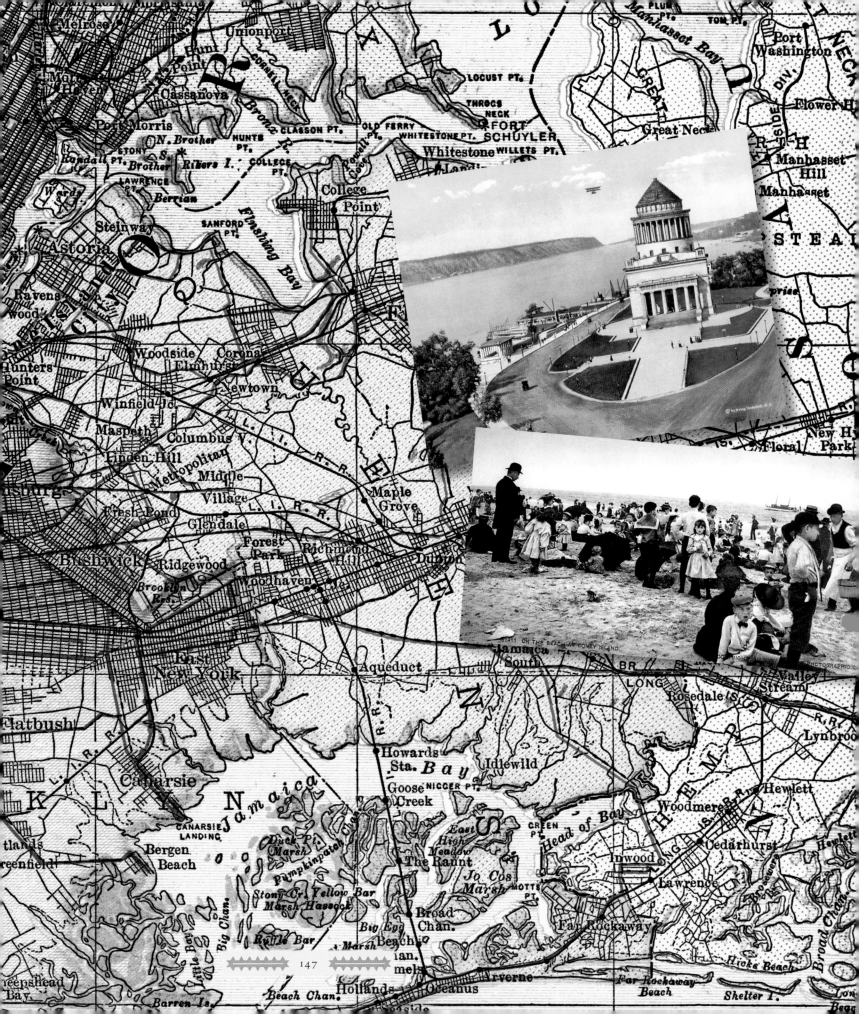

ON THE BEACH AT CONEY ISLAND.

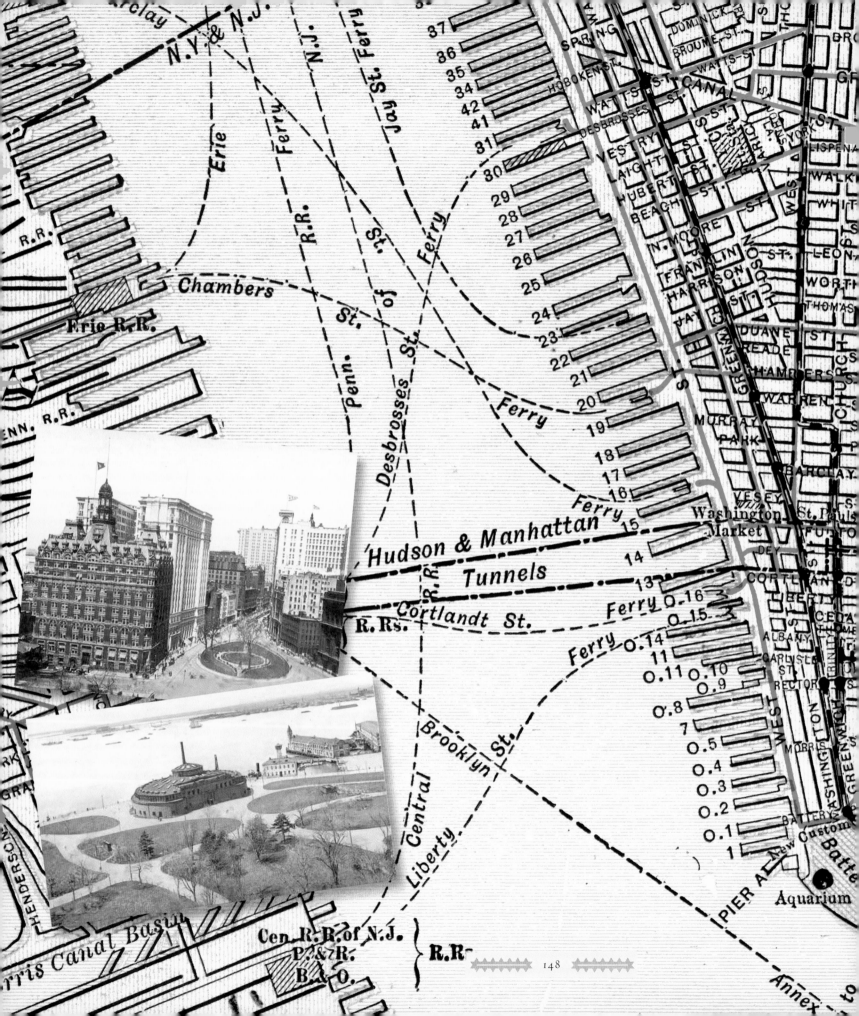

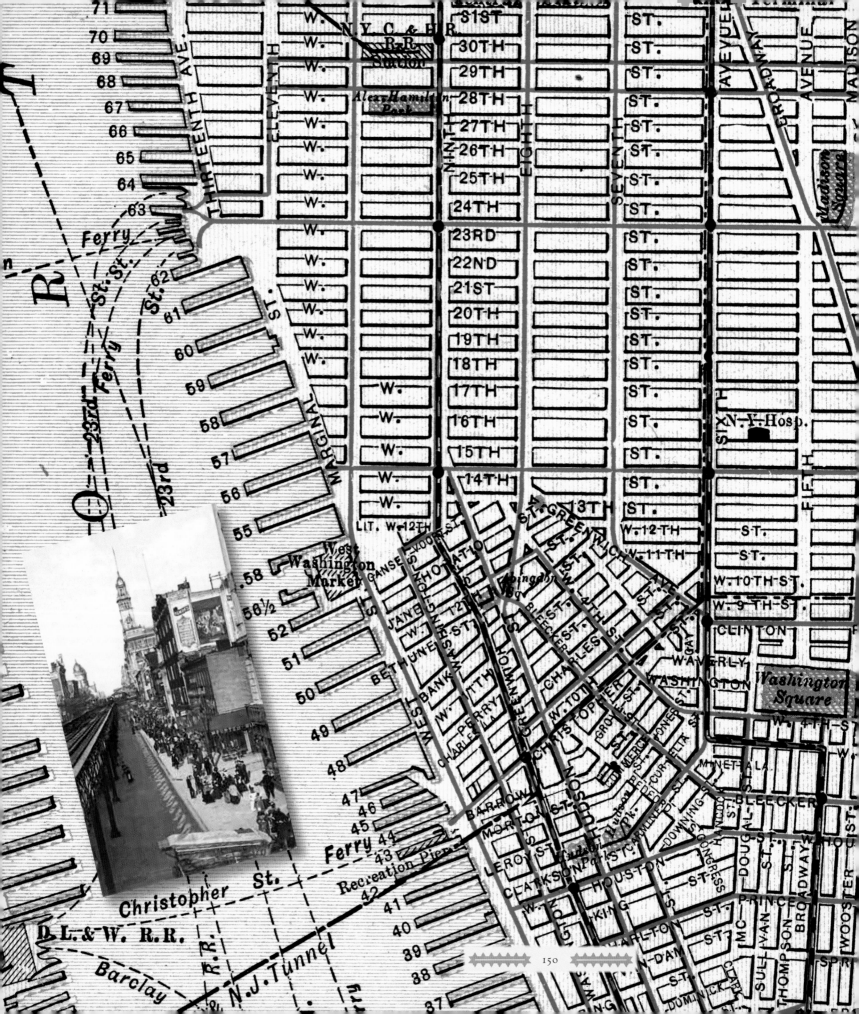

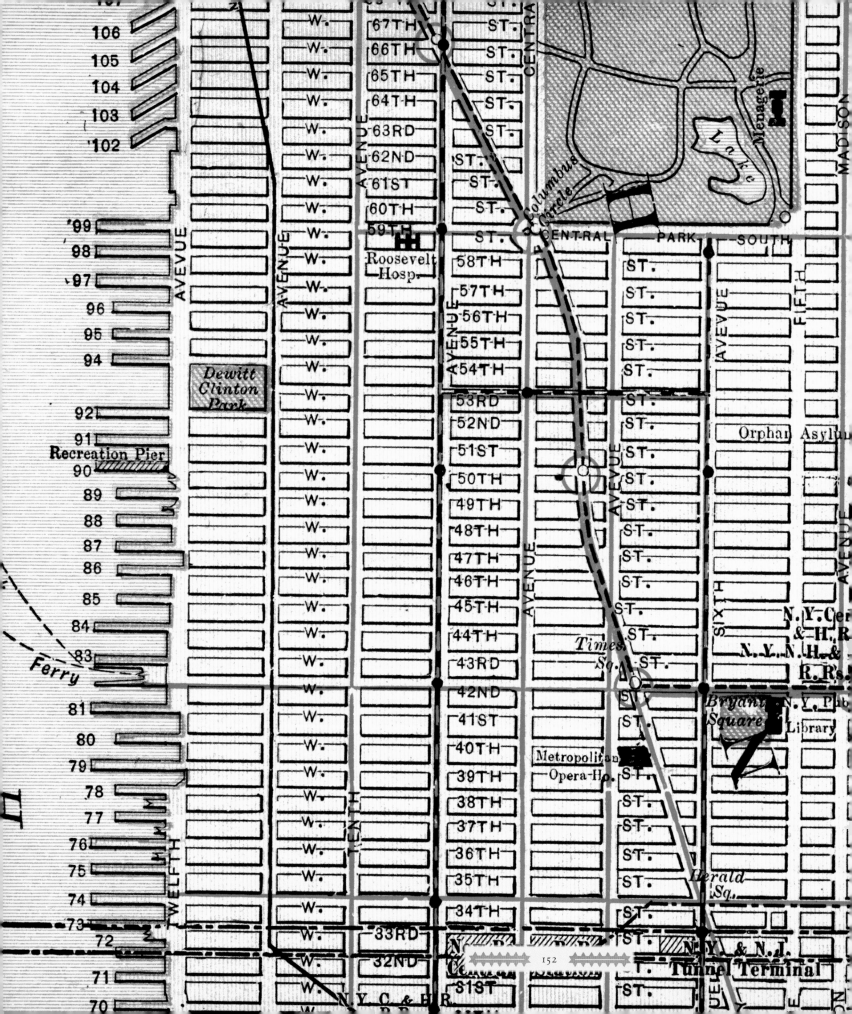

Entrance to Central Park, 59th Street and 8th Avenue.

NEW YORK
CENTRAL
& HUDSON RIVER
· R·R·

Form A.
Mileage Book No. C 29413
(1000 MILES.)

ISSUED TO
M A. W. Mills
Address Auburn
ny

Not good unless
stamped here.   DATE OF SALE

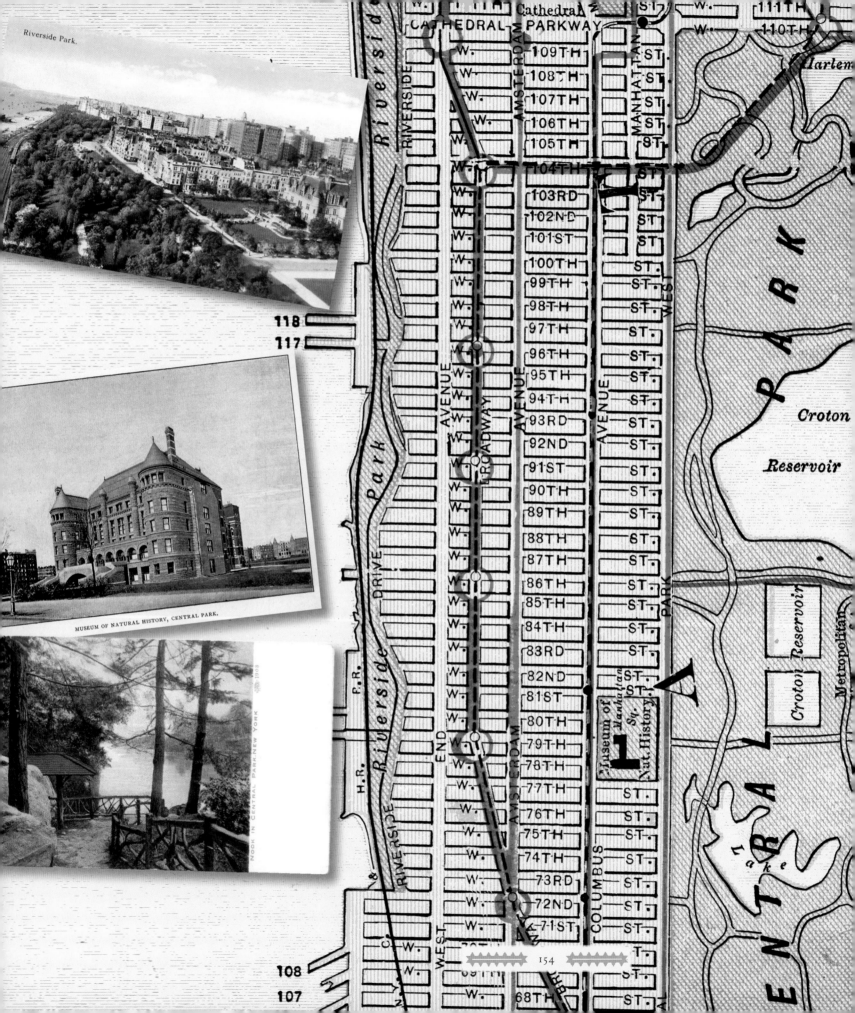

Riverside Park.

MUSEUM OF NATURAL HISTORY, CENTRAL PARK.

NOOK IN CENTRAL PARK, NEW YORK.

154

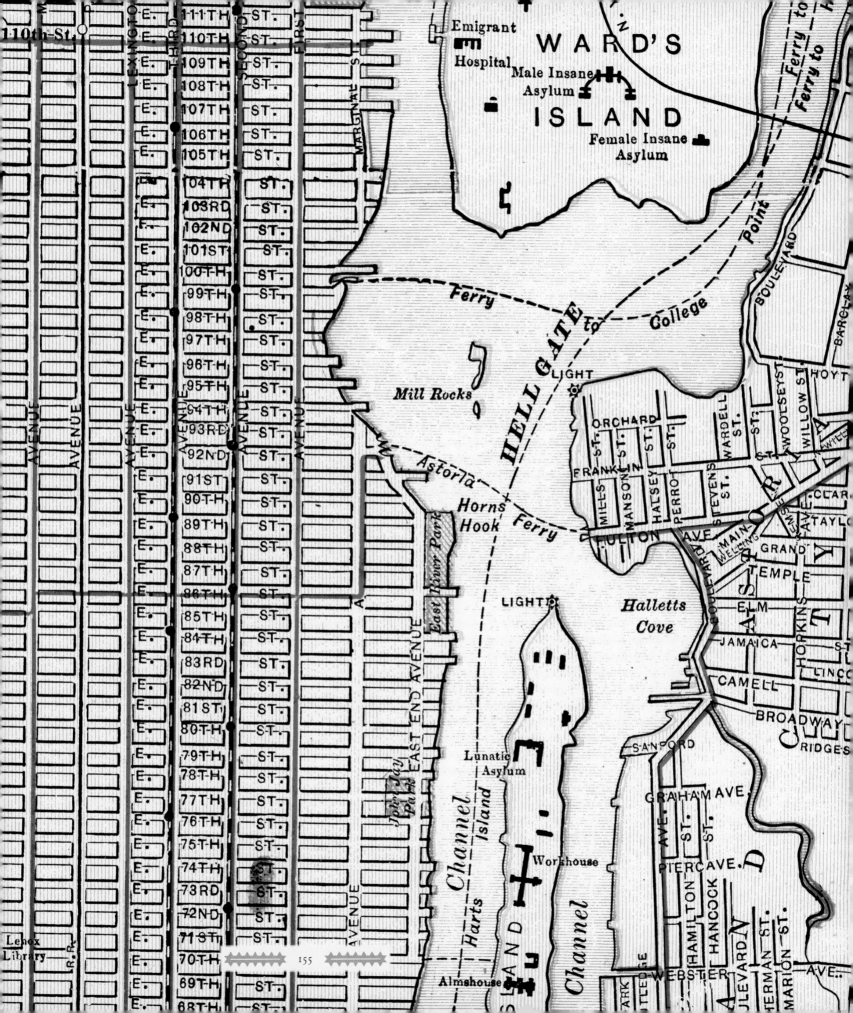

ELLIS ISLAND
U.S. Immigrant
Landing Sta.

Ellis Island Ferry

Bedloe's (Liberty) Island Ferry

Statue of Liberty

Castle William

GOVERNORS
ISLAND

Ft
Columbus

Buttermilk   Channel

Ferry to St. George Staten Island

Whitehall St. & 39th (Brooklyn) Ferry

E   R   I   E

Atlantic   Basin

North Pier

South Pier

Erie
Basin

GOWANUS
BAY

Post Card

AUTHORIZED BY ACT OF CONGRESS OF MAY 19–1898.
("POST CARTE – POSTAL CARD – CARTE POSTALE.")

Place Postage
Stamp Here

Domestic and
Canada
One Cent

Foreign
Two Cents

Miss M. Young
Villa Bank
Scotland
South Beach
Troon

S SIDE FOR THE ADDRESS

STATUE OF LIBERTY   NEW YORK
202

PUB. BY ILLUSTRATED POSTAL CARD CO., NEW YORK.

GREENWOOD
CEMETERY

SOUTH ENTRANCE, PROSPECT PARK, BROOKLYN.

BAEDEKER'S UNITED STATES

The wealthy and inquisitive world traveler of 1910 went nowhere without a Baedeker. The famous series of red-bound guides, published in Leipzig, began in 1861 with a guide to the Rhein. It was not until 1893, however, that the first *Baedeker's United States* was published, reaching its fourth edition in 1909.

The street map of New York reproduced here is from the 1904 edition. Interestingly, it still shows the pre–Brooklyn Bridge street layout overlaid by the black outline of the 1883 structure, suggesting that the base plan was unchanged from the first edition.

A New World of Color Printing

The sophisticated urbanites of 1910 New York loved color in their books, magazines, and advertising—and great strides in printing and ink technology allowed them to have it, breaking free of the limitations of the monotone pages of their parents' generation with their woodcuts and steel engravings. Many of these developments came from Europe, particularly from Germany, where by the turn of the nineteenth century there was a lucrative industry in color postcards, greeting cards, and books containing dozens of color illustrations.

The challenge and promise of color were quickly taken up in the United States—especially in New York and Chicago where presses started using the latest technology to print color plates for a wide range of reference books.

Until the early 1890s, anyone who wanted to print a color image had to design the images in such a way

Opposite page: (top) painting by Digby Chandler, engraved by Leopold and Crowe, New York, and printed in three colors, *Graphic Arts and Crafts Year Book, 1907*; (bottom left) jug and vase, three-color halftone plates engraved by Barnes Crosby Co., *Graphic Arts and Crafts Year Book, 1908*; (bottom right) "Naval Arch, Madison Square," an 1898 photochrome.

This page: (top) *Rocky Mountain Views*, made exclusively for the Inter-State Co., Denver, and published by Smith-Brooks in 1914; (center right) the view from the book is of Glenwood Springs; (top right) a still life of fruit by Stockinger Photo Engraving and Printing Co., Brooklyn, from *Graphic Arts and Crafts Year Book 1911–12*; (bottom) frontispiece from *Graphic Arts and Crafts Year Book, 1907*.

that the different colors—each printed from its own plate—could easily be separated from each other. Many ways were developed to create subtlety in the use of color, including engraving fine detail into each color plate, using separate plates for different tones of the same color, and hand-finishing each plate after it had been printed. Even so, most color printing in 1900 was fairly crude, and it is clear—especially under the magnifying glass—that the drive for realistic color still had some way to go.

The best color printing in 1910, however, was stunning. In the period between 1900 and 1914, before war dried up ink and machinery supplies from Germany to the rest of the world, printing in color reached a level not to be attained again until the 1960s.

How did they achieve this quality? It is important to remember that outdoor color photography as we

To Those Who Love Their Work

know it, using color film to photograph places and people, was not invented until the 1930s. However, from about 1890 onward, several processes for making color photographs of inanimate objects in a studio setting were well advanced, and Edwardian photographers were amazingly inventive.

One of the greatest pioneers was a German emigrant, Carl Hentschel, who in the 1890s patented the Hentschel Colourtype Process. Hentschel developed a massive camera that used three color filters—red, green, and blue—to capture simultaneous images of any flat color original. At the same time, developments such as the halftone screen, which allowed color gradation to be printed as an almost imperceptible regular pattern of different-sized dots onto paper, enabled photographed images to be transferred to paper, both in black and white and in the new three-color process method.

It was now possible to photograph flat objects like paintings, or small groups of objects in a studio setting, in color. And it was possible to use those images,

Carl Hentschel (top) and the original "three men in a boat" (below)—Carl Hentschel, George Wingrave, and Jerome K. Jerome.

The chromographoscope, invented by Louis Ducos du Hauron in 1874, was a dual-purpose machine. It could be used as a camera or as an additive viewer.

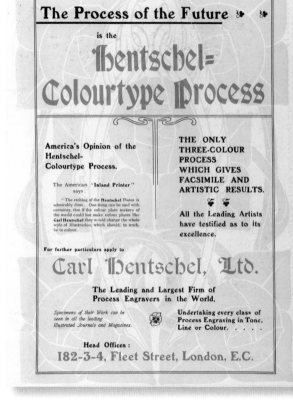

separated into their three component process colors, to print color images. It was impossible, however, to make color photographs of the wider world—of cities, mountains, and crowds of people. Yet once they had a taste of color postcards and color pictures in books, those who could afford to buy such relatively expensive luxuries wanted as much color as they could get.

The images in this book demonstrate the many ways in which inventors, photographers, and publishers in 1910 strove to give their customers what they so craved: the real world on the printed page in full color.

THE HENTSCHEL THREE-COLOR PROCESS
Carl Hentschel moved to London from the Russian-Polish city of Lodz with his family in 1868 when he was four years old. Like his father, he became an engraver, and by 1900 was an important figure both in color

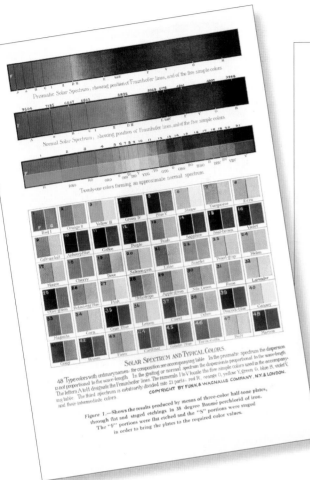

Figure 1.—Shows the results produced by means of three-color half-tone plates, through flat and staged etchings in 38 degree Baumé perchloride of iron. The "F" portions were flat etched and the "S" portions were staged in order to bring the plates to the required color values.

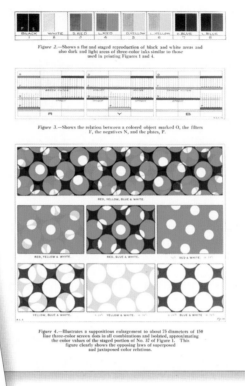

Figure 2.—Shows a flat and staged reproduction of black and white areas and also dark and light areas of three-color inks similar to those used in printing Figures 1 and 4.

Figure 3.—Shows the relation between a colored object marked O, the filters F, the negatives N, and the plates, P.

Figure 4.—Illustrates a suppositious enlargement to about 75 diameters of 150 line three-color screen dots in all combinations and isolated, approximating the color values of the staged portion of No. 37 of Figure 1. This figure clearly shows the opposing laws of superposed and juxtaposed color relations.

Solar spectrum and typical colors (far left), produced by three-color halftone plates and an enlargement of three-color screen dot process charts (left), both from *Graphic Arts and Crafts Year Book*, 1910.

A wonderful sample of design and color lithographic printing (above) by Strobridge Lithographing Co., Cincinnati, from *The Graphic Arts and Crafts Year Book*, 1908.

printing and in London's social life. As well as being an active advocate of his innovative printing process, he was a founding member of several clubs, including the Playgoer's Club, and as a great friend of Jerome K. Jerome, was the model for Harris in Jerome's *Three Men in a Boat*.

Although not the inventor of the three-color halftone process (it had already been developed by Frenchmen Louis du Hauron and Charles Cros, and American Frederick Ives in the 1870s), Hentschel's company led the way in using the method on a commercial scale.

The process is well described in Burch's 1906 book *Colour Printing and Colour Printers*: "Once the principle is accepted that any combination of colours can be resolved into its primary elements, it remains only for the photographer to obtain three negatives which automatically dissect the original, making three

Color wheel (left), illustrating an essay entitled "The Science and Practice of Color Mixing" by C. G. Zander, from *Graphic Arts and Crafts Year Book*, 1907.

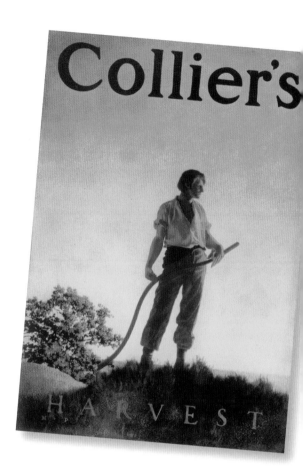

distinct photographic records of the reds, yellows and blues which enter into the composition. The result is obtained by the use of transparent screens of coloured pigment or liquid, 'light filters' as they are technically termed, placed in front of the lens. These filters admit any two of the primary colours and absorb the other one. Three separate screens are employed, each with the lines ruled at a different angle, and when the negative records of the colour analysis are obtained, the three photographs are converted into printing surfaces."

COLOR PRINTING IN AMERICA

American printers were generally a decade or so behind their European counterparts. What they lacked in experience, they easily made up with enthusiasm. By 1910 the gap had narrowed to the extent that the best North American color printing was some of the highest quality in the world.

Three-color reproduction of art glass domes (above) by Barnes Crosby Co., from *The Graphic Arts and Crafts Year Book, 1909*; Collier's *The National Weekly* (top right), drawn by Maxfield Parrish and printed in three colors, from *The Graphic Arts and Crafts Year Book*, 1907.

A portrait in four colors (below), from a painting by C.F. Underwood, printed by the Zeese Wilkinson Co., New York, *Graphic Arts and Crafts Year Book, 1910*; advertisement (right) for Barnes-Crosby, *Graphic Arts and Crafts Year Book*, 1907.

In Europe, the annual showcase for printers' color output was *The Process Year-Book*, first published in 1895 by the pioneering printing supplies company Penrose. The American equivalent, *The Graphic Arts and Crafts Year Book*, edited by the innovative and forward-looking printer Joseph Meadon, was first published by the Republican Publishing Co. of Hamilton, Ohio, in 1907. A number of trade magazines, such as *The Printing Art* and *The American Printer*, regularly published striking color examples, but *The Graphic Arts and Crafts Year Book* showcased only the crème de la crème—color printing that would not be equaled until four-color process printing came of age in the 1970s.

COLOR POSTCARDS

The first decade of the twentieth century was the high tide of the postcard craze, which used the new technologies of color printing and the one-cent postcard postage rate to fill living rooms with pictures from all over the world. On March 1, 1907, the United States Postal Service gave in to public pressure to

The Dutch Garden, Van Cortlandt Park, New York (below), a postcard sent in October 1908 to Niagara Falls; Old Lorillard Mansion, Bronx Park (right), a postcard produced by the Souvenir Post Card Co., New York and Berlin, and printed in Berlin; a bird's-eye view of Madison Square Garden (far right), sent to an address in Glasgow, Scotland, in June 1911; Chinatown (below) by Brown Brothers, printed in Germany.

allow more than just the address written on the back, which allowed publishers to use all of the picture side to display their design.

Postcard publishers rapidly increased production to fill the demand for postcards, as these cards were the one product line that constantly pushed color printing to the limits of what was achievable. Many color postcards, even of less-familiar New York scenes, were printed in Germany, or by American companies with German origins.

In the first decades of the postcard's life, there were three ways of producing a color image. You either started with a real black-and-white photograph, then added subtle layers of color to indicate water or a sunset, or you used traditional color engravers to create separated color designs from scratch, or used the new three-color process to photograph painted originals. It was this third option that allowed postcard companies to expand so rapidly, and they were quick to commission artists to create series of paintings specifically for reproduction as postcards.

Photochromes: West Street, New York (left);
St. Paul's Chapel, New York (below left);
Washington Bridge and Speedway (below).

PHOTOCHROMES

Of all the methods for colorizing photographic images before outdoor color photography, the photochrome process was the most successful. The brilliantly colored prints displayed at the 1889 Paris Exposition by the Swiss company Orell Füssli and Co. won a gold medal and thrilled those who saw them with their realism. Only three companies—Füssli's own Photoglob in Switzerland, Photochrome in Britain, and the Detroit Printing Company in the United States—were ever licensed to use the "secret" technique, which by 1910 had resulted in more than 13,000 color images of every corner of Europe, the landmarks of North America, India, and North Africa.

Each photochrome involved intensive labor, an artistic eye, and ideally, an accurate record of what colors were actually present in the scene portrayed. A film negative was used as the basis for creating a series

Photochromes of Coney Island bathers, 1902 (below); and St. Paul's building, 1898 (far right); 1900 advertisement for a play at Coney Island (right); detail from a sunset view from the Manhattan Battery, 1901 (below right).

51410 THE BATHERS AT CONEY ISLAND.   COPYRIGHT, 1902, BY DETROIT PHOTOGRAPHIC CO.

of lithographic plates—flat pieces of stone quarried in Bavaria and coated with asphaltum, one stone for each color. The negative had to be retouched by hand for each color—sometimes fourteen different colors were being used—and then the stone was exposed to sunlight for several hours before it was developed with turpentine. Each stone was hand-finished with the additional development of chosen areas and fine pumice powder before being etched in acid to reveal the image ready for printing. Special semitransparent inks

were then used to transfer the image from the stones onto smooth paper, and finally each printed image was varnished to bring out its depth and richness.

The Detroit Photographic Company published around a hundred photochrome images of New York, which were available to the public as prints for framing and as postcards. These and more than five thousand other photochromes can be seen online at http://www.ushistoricalarchive.com/photochroms/index.html.

PAINTING LOCATIONS

This page lists the locations, as far as the publishers are aware, of all the main paintings reproduced in this volume. We are grateful for permission to reproduce these paintings, and if we have inadvertently misattributed any locations or ownerships, we shall be pleased to correct these details in future editions.

Given such a wonderful collection of images of New York a hundred years ago, it is sad that so few of the originals can be seen by the public—even the Metropolitan dedicates only a small gallery at the rear of the building to the American Impressionists, and none of the paintings included here is on permanent display. We hope that bringing this collection together will help spark a renewed interest in these important painters, as significant in their context as the great European Impressionists.

Page	Title	Date	Artist	Location/source of painting
26	Manhattan's Misty Sunset	1911	Frederick Childe Hassam	Butler Institute of American Art
28	Lower Manhattan	1907	Frederick Childe Hassam	Willard Straight Hall Collection, Cornell University
30	View of Wall Street	n.d.	Colin Campbell Cooper	Private collection, image courtesy of Sotheby's New York
32	Mountains of Manhattan	1903	Colin Campbell Cooper	Collection of the City of Santa Barbara, California
34	Cliffs of Manhattan	1903	Colin Campbell Cooper	Collection of the City of Santa Barbara, California
36	October Haze, Manhattan	1910	Frederick Childe Hassam	Private collection, image courtesy of Sotheby's New York
38	St. Paul's Chapel	1890	William Louis Sonntag Jr.	Private collection, image courtesy of Godel & Co. Fine Art
40	Brooklyn Bridge in Winter	1904	Frederick Childe Hassam	The Telfair Academy of Arts and Sciences, Savannah, Georgia
42	A Winter Day on Brooklyn Bridge	1892	Frederick Childe Hassam	Private collection, image courtesy of Berry-Hill Galleries, New York
44	The Brooklyn Bridge	1895	William Louis Sonntag Jr.	Museum of the City of New York
46	The Bowery at Night	1895	William Louis Sonntag Jr.	Museum of the City of New York
48	Washington Arch, Spring	1890	Frederick Childe Hassam	The Metropolitan Museum of Art, New York
50	Fifth Avenue at Washington Square	1891	Frederick Childe Hassam	Thyssen-Bornemisza Collection
52	Lower Fifth Avenue	1890	Frederick Childe Hassam	Private collection, image courtesy of Christie's New York
54	Rain Storm, Union Square	1890	Frederick Childe Hassam	Museum of the City of New York
56	Early Evening, Union Square	n.d.	Frederick Childe Hassam	Private collection, image courtesy of Christie's New York
58	Union Square in Spring	1896	Frederick Childe Hassam	Smith College Museum of Art, Northampton, Massachusetts
60	Winter in Union Square	1890	Frederick Childe Hassam	The Metropolitan Museum of Art, New York
62	Fifth Avenue	1919	Frederick Childe Hassam	The Cleveland Museum of Art
64	Fifth Avenue in Winter	1892	Frederick Childe Hassam	The Carnegie Museum of Art, Pittsburgh, Pennsylvania
66	A Spring Morning	1891	Frederick Childe Hassam	Private collection, image courtesy of Berry-Hill Galleries, New York
68	View of Broadway and Fifth Avenue	1890	Frederick Childe Hassam	The Metropolitan Museum of Art, New York
70	Flat Iron Building	1904	Colin Campbell Cooper	Dallas Museum of Art
72	The Metropolitan Tower	1917	Colin Campbell Cooper	Private collection
74	Spring Morning in the Heart of the City	1890	Frederick Childe Hassam	The Metropolitan Museum of Art, New York
76	Fifth Avenue	1906	Colin Campbell Cooper	The New York Historical Society
78	The Manhattan Club	1891	Frederick Childe Hassam	Santa Barbara Museum of Art
80	The El	n.d.	Frederick Childe Hassam	Private collection, image courtesy of Christie's New York
82	Broadway and 42nd Street	1902	Frederick Childe Hassam	The Metropolitan Museum of Art, New York
84	Times Square	1905	Frederick Childe Hassam	Private collection
86	Horse-Drawn Cabs at Evening	1890	Frederick Childe Hassam	Private collection, image courtesy of Berry-Hill Galleries, New York
88	New York Public Library	1912	Colin Campbell Cooper	Private collection
90	Old Grand Central Station	1906	Colin Campbell Cooper	Montclair Art Museum, Montclair, New Jersey
92	The Cathedral and Fifth Avenue	1893	Frederick Childe Hassam	Private collection, image courtesy of Christie's New York
94	Cathedral Spires, Spring Morning	1900	Frederick Childe Hassam	Private collection, image courtesy of Christie's Images
96	Sunday on Fifth Avenue	n.d.	Frederick Childe Hassam	Private collection, image courtesy of James Graham & Sons, New York
98	Snowstorm, Fifth Avenue	1907	Frederick Childe Hassam	Private collection, image courtesy of Christie's New York
100	Late Afternoon, New York	1900	Frederick Childe Hassam	The Brooklyn Museum
102	Columbus Circle	1923	Colin Campbell Cooper	Norton Museum of Art, West Palm Beach, Florida
104	Nightfall Over Columbus Circle	n.d.	William Louis Sonntag Jr.	Private collection, image courtesy of Godel & Co. Fine Art
106	Church of the Paulist Fathers	n.d.	Frederick Childe Hassam	Private collection, image courtesy of Christie's New York
108	Across the Park	1904	Frederick Childe Hassam	Private collection, image courtesy of Christie's New York
110	Central Park	1892	Frederick Childe Hassam	Private collection
112	Lake for Miniature Yachts	1888	William Merritt Chase	Private collection
114	Central Park	1927	Colin Campbell Cooper	Private collection
116	A Bit of the Terrace	1890	William Merritt Chase	Private collection
118	Terrace at the Mall, Central Park	1888	William Merritt Chase	Private collection
120	Summer in the Park	n.d.	Frederick Childe Hassam	Private collection, image courtesy of Christie's New York
122	The Common, Central Park	1889	William Merritt Chase	Private collection
124	The Hovel and the Skyscraper	1904	Frederick Childe Hassam	Private collection
126	Springtime, West 78th Street	n.d.	Frederick Childe Hassam	Private collection
128	Woman on a Dock, Rotten Row, Brooklyn	1886	William Merritt Chase	Private collection, image courtesy of Berry-Hill Galleries, New York
130	In Brooklyn Navy Yard	1887	William Merritt Chase	Private collection
132	Harbour Scene, Brooklyn Docks	1886	William Merritt Chase	Yale University Art Gallery
134	The East River	1886	William Merritt Chase	Private collection, image courtesy of Thomas Colville Fine Arts
136	Boat House, Prospect Park	1888	William Merritt Chase	Private collection
138	Prospect Park, Brooklyn	1887	William Merritt Chase	Private collection, image courtesy of Sotheby's New York
140	A City Park	1887	William Merritt Chase	The Art Institute of Chicago
142	Tompkins Park	1887	William Merritt Chase	Colby College Museum of Art
144	Wash Day, Brooklyn	1886	William Merritt Chase	Private collection

Sources, Notes, and Captions

The images used to complement the paintings come from a wide variety of sources, including books, postcards, museums, and libraries. They include photochromes, ephemera, advertisements, and maps of the period. The photochromes, and more than 5,000 others, can be seen online at www.ushistoricalarchive.com/photochroms/index.html.

New York is fortunate in that it has several important and wide-ranging public archives of historical material, as well as a public library system where public access is taken seriously enough both to digitize entire collections and to make them publicly available via the Internet. For New York City material, the most important is the New York Public Library, whose Web site at www.nypl.org leads to a treasure trove of original period material, collected over the years by proud New Yorkers who believed their city to be the best place in the world to live and work. Sources marked (NYPL) are from this rich vein.

The large colored numbers refer to the plate numbers.

1 Top left: *Between Daylight and Darkness* (1909), painted by Edward Redfield (private collection). Middle: New York Harbor at sunset, a 1905 postcard (NYPL). Bottom right: Shipping at East River Docks, New York, *c.* 1910 (NYPL). Bottom left: *Sunset*, July 1903, painted by "Bru" (NYPL).

2 Top left: New York Stock Exchange, 1910 postcard (NYPL). Bottom left: Gillender Building, 1906 postcard. Below middle: 1914 postcard of Nassau Street North from Wall Street, featuring the Gillender Building (note the new building to the right of Gillender Building, absent in the earlier postcard). Below right: red and blue New York stock transfer tax stamps, early 1900s. Middle right: Wall Street postcard showing Sub-Treasury Building. Bottom: ten-dollar note, 1907.

3 Left: Hudson River Terminal Buildings, 1908 postcard. Middle: Municipal Building, from *New York: Wonder City*, published in 1919 by the American Art Publishing Company. Right: Woolworth Building, from *New York: Wonder City*.

4 Left: Singer Building, from *New York: Greatest City*, produced by F. W. Woolworth Co. in 1912. Middle: East River and Harbor from Brooklyn Bridge *c.* 1899 (NYPL). Right: *The Singer Building from Brooklyn Bridge* by Rachel Robinson Elmer (1878–1919), from *Art Lover's New York* published by P. F. Volland Company (NYPL).

5 Bottom right: title page from *Interborough Rapid Transit, the New York Subway: Its Construction and Equipment*, published in 1904 by the New York Interborough Rapid Transit Company (NYPL). Left: Mutual Life advertisement from *King's Photographic Views of New York*, Moses King, Boston, 1895. Top: 1905 postcard of Park Row.

6 Top left: Joseph Pulitzer, an Allen and Ginter cigarette card from a series called *The New York World* (NYPL). Middle: Municipal Building, Newspaper Row, 1905 postcard front and back. Below right: Park Row Building, a 1910 postcard.

7 Bottom: outside St. Paul's Chapel, during the "One Year After 9/11 Exhibition," photograph by Leo Sorel (www.saintpaulschapel.org). Bottom middle: railings outside St. Paul's, also by Leo Sorel. Top left: group of skyscrapers, St. Paul's Chapel and churchyard, postcard (NYPL). Right: Washington's pew in St. Paul's Church, 1789, a lithograph by A. Weingärtner, from *Manual of the Corporation of the City of New York* (NYPL).

8 Bottom: Brooklyn Bridge, seen from New York, from *The Earth and Its Inhabitants*, Universal Geography, Vol XVI, published by J. S. Virtue in 1895. Right: 1905 postcard of Williamsburg Bridge. Left: winter outfits, 1913 (NYPL).

9 Bottom right: *On Brooklyn Bridge, New York Side*, from *50 Glimpses of New York*, Mercantile Illustrating Co., 1893. Bottom left: postcard of the cables, Brooklyn Bridge. Top left: *Winter in the Great Metropolis*, 1895 (NYPL). The text accompanying the image reads: "In Maloney's 'Family Entrance,' as the night draws on apace, Roundsman Grady of the Finest goes to irrigate his face. On his box the sleepy cabby dreams and gets an awful scare, dreams a passenger escaped him without paying double fare. At the curb Cornelius Epstein feels the cold, but isn't blue, for he sells a 'bair o' shoestrings' once in every hour or two. Homeward trips the weary actress, bold and brave she fears no harm. That's her Living Picture costume in the bundle 'neath her arm. She's as proud as any princess—Daisy Heiress, wrapped in furs—Lord De Brokeleigh isn't pretty, but she's bought him, and he's her's. Down the street the chilly actor trudges on for many a block, 'I'm in luck,' he says, devoutly, 'that this coat is out of hock!' Oft the car-conductor shivers, but his mind is free from cares, for he never knocks down people nights—he only 'knocks down' fares. On the corner 'Auntie' Mooney, o'er her lack of trade doth grieve. She's been in the apple business since the days of Mother Eve. Chimmy Reagan, selling papers, bundled up in all his wraps, has but one regret in winter: it's too cold for 'shooting craps.' Jan. 12, 1895." Top right: *Daily Graphic*, May 24, 1883, commemorating the opening of the Brooklyn Bridge.

10 Bottom: *Brooklyn Bridge at Night* (1909) by Edward Redfield (private collection). Left: 1906 postcard of Brooklyn Bridge. Right: steamship advertisement from *King's Photographic Views of New York*, Moses King, Boston, 1895.

11 Bottom: "The Bowery," an 1898 photochrome. Below right: a 1906 postcard of the Bowery and elevated road. Top right: the Bowery, from a pack of souvenir New York view playing cards published by A. C. Bossleman and Co., New York, *c.* 1900.

12 Top left: *Fifth Avenue through Washington Arch*, a pastel drawing by Joseph Pennell from *The New New York: A Commentary on the Place and the People* by John C. Van Dyke, Macmillan, 1909. Bottom left: souvenir playing cards box and cards, as in the notes for plate 11. Top right: Washington Arch by C. Moore Park. Bottom right: photograph of the temporary arch (NYPL).

13 Bottom left: "Washington Square North, numbers 121–125," *c.* 1935, a photograph by Berenice Abbott (NYPL). Middle: women's blouses and parasols, 1910s (NYPL). Right: a four-color plate produced by Barnes Crosby Company, Chicago, from *Graphic Arts and Crafts Year Book*, 1910.

14 Left: *Fifth Avenue on Sunday*, from *Select New York: 100 Albertype Illustrations*, published by Witteman in 1890 (NYPL). Top: *Church of the Ascension, Fifth Avenue*, painted by J. Well (private collection). Right: "First Presbyterian Church," a 1900 photograph (NYPL).

15 Top left: advertisement for Kuppenheimer coats, 1906 (NYPL). Middle: McClures in the 1900s (NYPL). Right: "Brentano's Periodicals, Books, Photographs and Stationery," from *King's Photographic Views of New York*, Moses King, Boston, 1895.

16 Bottom: Union Square *c.* 1870, from *Picturesque America*, Vol II, D. Appleton and Co., 1874. Top left: "The New Store of Messrs Tiffany and Co., Union Square, 1870," by John Kellum (NYPL). Top right: half-tone engraving by the Scientific Engraving Co., New York, from *Graphic Arts and Crafts Year Book*, 1911–12. Right: "In Front of Tiffany's, Union Square, 1899," from *The New Metropolis: Memorable Events of Three Centuries*, Appleton, 1899.

17 Bottom left: proposed plan improvements of Union Park, Spangenberg, 1871 (NYPL). Top left: Spring and Summer Season, 1909, catalog cover from *The Graphic Arts and Crafts Year Book*, 1910. Right: Union Square, from a 1906 map (NYPL).

18 Bottom left: *Century Magazine* cover (NYPL). Bottom: Union Square North from the Morton House, a 1910 postcard. Top: Domestic Sewing Machine Co. Building, 1872, by S. Fox (NYPL). Top right: Grace Church, New York, by Irving Underhill, published by H. Finkelstein and Son for the American Art Publishing Co. (NYPL).

19 Top right: *The Chart Expert on Change*, a drawing by Hy. Mayer from *The Real New York* by Rupert Hughes, Smart Set Publishing Co., 1904. Main image: Fifth Avenue from *New York: The Wonder City*, American Art Publishing Company, 1919.

20 Bottom left: *Winter, New York City, 17 February 1900* by Everett Shinn (NYPL). Middle: "A Fifth Avenue Stage, New York," a photochrome by the Detroit Photographic Co. (NYPL). Right: Santa Claus cover design by the Central Engraving Co., Ohio, from *The Graphic Arts Yearbook, 1909*.

21 Left: Advertisement for O'Neills, Importers and Retailers, Sixth Avenue, November 27, 1890 (NYPL). Middle: catalog cover in two colors, drawn and engraved by Barnes Crosby Co., from *Graphic Arts Year Book, 1909*. Top right: Church of the Holy Communion, from *Booth's History of New York*, Vol. 8, 1890. Bottom right: *Springtime*, a print by the Autogravure Co., from *The Graphic Arts and Crafts Year Book, 1911–12*.

22 Top left: *In This We Bury All Unkindness*, a President Cleveland illustration by Grimm (NYPL). Bottom left: R. Wallace Jewellers, next to the Victoria Hotel, from *King's Photographic Views of New York*, Moses King, Boston, 1895. Middle: color illustration of Madison Square, Broadway and Fifth Avenue (NYPL). Right: William Jenkins Worth (NYPL).

23 Bottom left: *The Flatiron on a Windy Day*, a drawing by Hy. Mayer from *The Real New York* by Rupert Hughes, the Smart Set Publishing Co., 1904. Top: the Flatiron Building being built in 1902, Detroit Photographic Co. (NYPL). Right: Flatiron Building, from *New York: Wonder City*, American Art Publishing Co., New York, 1919.

24 Top left: a 1907 illustration of the Filing Section, Metropolitan Life Insurance Co., New York (NYPL). Below left: frontispiece for a catalog, from *The Graphic Arts and Crafts Yearbook, 1911–12*. Main picture: Metropolitan Life Insurance Building, from *New York: Wonder City*. Below right: Madison Square Garden, a 1903 postcard by Irving Underhill.

25 Top left: daily menu for a 1907 dinner at the Fifth Avenue Hotel (NYPL). Bottom: Madison Square, from *Picturesque America*, Vol. II, D. Appleton and Co., 1874. Middle: Fifth Avenue Hotel, from *King's Photographic Views of New York*, Moses King, Boston, 1895. Right: Fifth Avenue Hotel dining room, 1859 (NYPL).

26 Left: Waldorf Astoria 1901 stereoscope (NYPL). Middle: the Waldorf Astoria, from *King's Photographic Views of New York*, Moses King, Boston, 1895. Bottom panorama, from left to right: West Thirty-third Street, Waldorf Astoria, West Thirty-fourth Street, Knickerbocker Trust Co., Aeolian Hall, Maillard's Confectioners, *From Start to Finish*, published in 1911 (NYPL).

27 Left: portrait of Alexander T. Stewart, from *Booth's History of New York*, Vol. 7, 1880 (NYPL). Top middle: residence of the late Alexander T. Stewart, 1876 (NYPL).

Bottom middle: 257 Broadway, the site of A. T. Stewart's first store, from *King's Photographic Views of New York*. Right: *St. Mark's Church, Tenth Street and Second Avenue*, an illustration by Charles F. Flower, from *Old Landmarks of New York* (NYPL).

28 Top left: holly, printed and embossed by Crescent Embossing Co., Plainfield, New Jersey, from *Graphic Arts and Crafts Year Book, 1908*. Bottom left: Herald Square, Sixth Avenue Broadway and Thirty-fifth Street, 1898 (NYPL). Bottom right: elevated railroad curve at 110th Street, a c. 1900 postcard.

29 Left: cover design from the January edition of the *Cosmopolitan*, from *The Graphic Arts and Crafts Year Book, 1911–12*. Middle: Longacre Square, a Detroit Publishing postcard (NYPL). Right: Times Square by night, from a folding view book of New York City produced by the Success Postal Card Co., New York.

30 Top left: a 1910 postcard of Times Square (NYPL). Below left: New Year card, c. 1905, front and back. Bottom right: Times Square on election night, from the pack of souvenir playing cards by A. C. Bosselman and Co. Right: a Joseph Pennell pastel of the Times Building, from *The New New York: A Commentary on the Place and the People* by John C. Van Dyke, Macmillan, 1909.

31 Top left: "Hansom Cab, New York," by Alice Austen, a gelatin silver print c. 1896 (NYPL). Top right: Broadway and Fourteenth Street, Domestic Sewing Machine Building, Longley Bros. Woolens, Demarest Building, Crawford Shoes (NYPL). Below: *Harper's* magazine cover by Edward Penfield (NYPL).

32 Top left: a 1911 illustration by Edward Penfield for the *Fall Style Book*, set in front of the Public Library (NYPL). Top right: a 1913 Knox Hats advertisement by Coles Phillips (NYPL). Below: the Public Library, from *New York: Wonder City*.

33 Top right: an illustration by Clarence Underwood from *Girls of Today*, Frederick A. Stokes Co., 1909. Below right: Grand Central Station by Herbert Kates, from *New York* by Ethel Fleming, A. & C. Black, 1929. Below: Grand Central, from *New York: Wonder City*.

34 Right: St. Patrick's Cathedral, a 1902–03 postcard by the Detroit Publishing Co. (NYPL). Top left: St. Patrick's Cathedral, from the pack of souvenir playing cards by A. C. Bosselman and Co. Bottom: St. Patrick's Cathedral before the spires were built (NYPL).

35 Left: St. Patrick's Cathedral, from *Folding View Book of New York City*, Success Postal Card Co., 1913. Middle: Sunday morning in Fifth Avenue, almost certainly in front of the cathedral, a 1900 postcard (NYPL). Right: interior of St. Patrick's Cathedral, Detroit Publishing Co., c. 1908 (NYPL).

36 Below right: 1904 fashions, from *Victorian and Edwardian Fashions from La Mode Illustrée*, edited by Joanne Olain, Dover, 1998. Left: Ernest Haskell, from *New York Sunday Journal*, October 1896 (NYPL). Top right: the Jewish Temple at Fifth Avenue and Forty-third Street, c. 1870, from *New York and Its Institutions 1609–1873* by J. F. Richmond.

37 Left: "Chestnut Stand in Downtown Manhattan," an 1890s photochrome. Middle: Fifth Avenue after a snowstorm, 1905, Detroit Photographic Co. (NYPL). Right: illustration by Clarence Underwood from *Girls of Today*, Frederick A. Stokes, 1909.

38 Left: fall and winter coats, from *The Graphic Arts and Crafts Year Book, 1910*. Top middle: Osborne Flats, Fifty-seventh Street and Seventh Avenue, 1887, from *Our Firemen: A Story of New York Fire Department* by A. Costello (NYPL). Middle below: laying the tubes for electricity in New York, 1882, by W. P. Snyder (NYPL). Below right: an Edward Penfield lithograph from *Harper's*, January 1897.

39 Left: a 1900 postcard of Columbus Circle (NYPL). Main picture: Columbus Circle, from *New York: Wonder City*.

40 Left: *Trolley Car Swing*, a 1912 illustration by Starmer, published by Jerome H. Remick and Co. (NYPL). Right: *Woman with Umbrella* by Charles Howard, cover from the *Boston Sunday Herald*, April 1895. Bottom: Worth Monument, a Robert N. Dennis stereoscopic view, c. 1870 (NYPL).

41 Middle top: Church of St. Paul the Apostle, from *King's Handbook*. Far left: dinner menu, Empire Hotel, 1900 (NYPL). Middle bottom: Isaac Hecker, the founder of the Paulists, a stained glass window from St. Paul's. Right: Isaac Hecker postcard image, c. 1910.

42 Left: *Woman and Horse* by Clarence Underwood, from *Girls of Today*, Frederick A. Stokes Co., 1909. Middle: 1908 map from Hammond's *Atlas of New York City and the Metropolitan District* of 1908. Right: "Donkeys in Central Park," Detroit Photographic Co., 1904 (NYPL).

43 Left: Central Park map by Foster and Reynolds, J. N. Matthews Co., Buffalo, c. 1910. Top right: 1910 postcard of the Swan Pond, Central Park. Middle: proposed conservatory, Central Park, an 1862 engraving by John William Orr (NYPL). Bottom: *In the Park*, an illustration by Hy. Mayer from *The Real New York*, 1904.

44 Top left: "The Dakota, between Seventy-second and Seventy-third Streets," c. 1890, from *Photographic Views of New York City* (NYPL). Bottom left: model yachts on the Lake, Central Park, from the Robert N. Dennis collection of stereoscopic views 1865–1905 (NYPL). Right: *Our Young Commodore* by Ida Waugh, c. 1910 (NYPL).

45 Top left: postcard of Hotel Majestic and Central Park West (NYPL). Bottom left: the Hotel Majestic, from *King's Photographic Views*, 1895. Bottom middle: cover design from *Outing* magazine, engraved in four colors, from the *Graphic Arts and Crafts Year Book, 1911–12*. Right: Cromwell Apartments, architect Emery Roth, from *Apartment Houses of the Metropolis*, 1908.

46 Left: front and back of a postcard, terraces in Central Park, posted July 27, 1908, to a Mrs. Goering in El Paso. Right: postcard of Bethesda Fountain, Central Park.

47 Left: "Angel of the Waters, Terrace Fountain, 1892," from *Photographic Views of New York City* (NYPL). Middle top: Bethesda Terrace, Central Park, from *New York: Greatest City*. Below: postcard of the terraces, Central Park.

48 Center: "Lovers with Rose," printed by the Zeese Wilkinson Co., New York, from *The Graphic Arts and Crafts Year Book*, 1910. Right: illustration by Clarence Underwood from *Girls of Today*, 1909.

49 Top left: sheep and lambs grazing on the Ball Ground, Central Park, from *Photographic Views of New York City* (NYPL). Center main picture: Navarro Apartment Buildings, from *King's Photographic Views*. Right: "Boys' Playground, Central Park, 1904," Detroit Photographic Co. (NYPL).

50 Left: building a skyscraper, *World's Work Magazine*, May 1903. Right: a Joseph Pennell pastel from *The New New York*.

51 Left: Theodore Dreiser, from the Pageant of America Collection (NYPL). Middle: Looking toward Grant's Tomb, Riverside Drive, Success Postal Card Co., *c.* 1900 (NYPL). Right: drawing by W. D. Goldbeck, made for Marshall Field and Co., from *The Graphic Arts and Crafts Year Book*, 1910.

52 Left: 1905 postcard of Navy Yard, Brooklyn. Below left: the Office, Brooklyn Navy Yard, 1904, Detroit Photographic Co. (NYPL). Right: 1904 postcard of the receiving ship *Vermont*, Brooklyn Navy Yard.

53 Left: detail of north Brooklyn, from Hammond's 1908 *Atlas of New York City and the Metropolitan District*. Bottom: Brooklyn Navy Yard, 1897 (NYPL). Right: Brooklyn Navy Yard looking southwest to commandant's house, National Archives and Record Administrations.

54 Bottom: East River from Brooklyn Bridge looking south, from *Views of Greater New York*, Isaac H. Blanchard Co., *c.* 1900. Top left: "The Wharves from Brooklyn Bridge, 1912," Detroit Photographic Co. (NYPL).

55 Bottom left: East River from Brooklyn Bridge looking north, from *Views of Greater New York*, Isaac H. Blanchard Co., *c.* 1900. Top middle: "Looking up the East River from the Foot of 59th Street," by Jules Vallée Guerin, *Scribner's Magazine*, October 1899. Right: postcard of Brooklyn Bridge.

56 Left: boat landing, Prospect Park, an 1890 stereoscope (NYPL). Middle: a postcard of the Prospect Park boat house. Right: an illustration by Clarence Underwood from *Girls of Today*, 1909.

57 Top left: a pastel drawing by Joseph Pennell from *The New New York*. Bottom: the Concert Grove steps of Main Terrace, Prospect Park, Brooklyn Historical Society. Right: detail from Hammond's 1908 *Atlas of New York City and the Metropolitan District*.

58 Left: interior of a greenhouse, a Prismaprint from *The Graphic Arts and Crafts Year Book, 1911–12*. Middle: Olmstead and Vaux's preliminary design for Tompkins Park, 1871, Brooklyn Museum of Art Library. Right: an illustration by Clarence Underwood from *Girls of Today*, 1909.

59 Top left: *I'm a Daisy* by Ida Waugh, published by L. Prang and Co., *c.* 1915 (NYPL). Bottom left: illustration by Katherine Richardson Wireman, from a 1910 article entitled "The Baby's Summer Wardrobe" by Ida Cleve Van Auken (NYPL). Right: Tompkins Park, from Hammond's 1908 *Atlas of New York City and the Metropolitan District*.

60 Top left: 1890 plan showing the Chase residence at 483 Marcy Avenue, Brooklyn Office of Assessors and Assessments. Below: washing strung across the backyards of tenement blocks, New York, an 1895 photochrome. Right: Fairbanks washing powder advertisement, *Munsey's Magazine*, 1889.

Bowling Green.

These notes refer to the map section on pages 146–61, describing the maps and the images on the maps reading from the top down. The large full-page maps on pages 146–59 are from *Hammond's Atlas of New York City and the Metropolitan District*, published by C. S. Hammond, 152 Broadway, New York, in 1908. The map on pages 160–61 is from *Baedeker's United States*, published by Karl Baedeker in 1904.

The numbers refer to the page numbers.

146 Main map: New York and vicinity. Left: *Hammond's Atlas* cover.

147 Top: Grant's Tomb, from *New York: Wonder City (Illustrating in Colors the Amazing Structures and Scenic Views of the World's Greatest City)*, published in 1919 by the American Art Publishing Company. Below: "On the Beach at Coney Island," a 1902 photochrome, published by the Detroit Photographic Company.

148 Main map: Manhattan Sheet 1 (South). Top: "Bowling Green and Lower Broadway," an 1899 photochrome. Below: "Battery Park and Upper Bay," an 1899 photochrome.

149 Brooklyn Bridge, a Currier and Ives print of 1893.

150 Main map: Manhattan Sheet 2 (Midtown). Left: "Sixth Avenue up from 14th Street," an 1898 photochrome.

152 Main map: Manhattan Sheet 3 (Central Park South).

153 Left: New York Central ticket book from 1904. Middle: New York subway token of 1906, with "New York City Transit Authority" written on the token. Right: entrance to Central Park, from *New York: The Greatest City*, F. W. Woolworth, published around 1910.

154 Main map: Manhattan Sheet 4 (Central Park North). Top: Riverside Park, from *New York: The Greatest City*. Middle: Museum of Natural History, from *50 Glimpses of New York*, Mercantile Illustrating Co., 1893. Bottom: nook in Central Park, a postcard dated 1908.

156 Main map: Brooklyn North. Postcard of the Statue of Liberty published by the Illustrated Postal Card Co. of New York. On the back of this card it says "Authorized by Act of Congress of May 19, 1898." The card was posted to Miss N. Young in Troon, Scotland, in April 1903.

158 Main map: Brooklyn South. A stereoscopic view from Ocean Hill of West Greenwood Cemetery, a stereoscope of around 1879.

159 South entrance of Prospect Park, from *Brooklyn: Views of Greater New York*, published by the Isaac H. Blanchard Company in around 1900.

160 Main map: central Manhattan, from the 1904 *Baedeker's United States*, whose cover is also illustrated.

BIBLIOGRAPHY

American Impressionism, William H. Gerdts, Abbeville Press, 1984.

The Architectural Guidebook to New York City, Francis Morrone, photography by James Iska, Gibbs-Smith, 1994; rev. ed. 2002.

The Birth of a Century: Early Color Photographs of America, Jim Hughes, with photographs by William Henry Jackson, and the Detroit Photographic Company, Tauris Parke, 1994.

Childe Hassam, American Impressionist, H. Barbara Weinberg, the Metropolitan Museum of Art/Yale University Press, 2004.

Childe Hassam's New York, Ilene Susan Fort, Chameleon Books, 1993.

Cityscapes: A History of New York in Images, Columbia University Press, 2001.

East Coast/West Coast and Beyond: Colin Campbell Cooper, American Impressionist, William H. Gerdts and Deborah Epstein Solon, Laguna Art Museum/the Irvine Museum/Hudson Hills Press, 2006.

Fifth Avenue: The Best Address, Jerry E. Patterson, Rizzoli, 1998.

Fifty Glimpses of New York, Mercantile Illustrating Company, 1893.

Girls of Today, Clarence F. Underwood, Frederick A. Stokes Company, 1909.

The Graphic Arts and Crafts Year Book, 1907, edited by Joseph Meadon, the Republican Publishing Company, 1907.

The Graphic Arts and Crafts Year Book, 1908, edited by Joseph Meadon, the Republican Publishing Company, 1908.

The Graphic Arts Year Book, 1909, edited by Joseph Meadon, the Republican Publishing Company, 1909.

The Graphic Arts and Crafts Year Book, 1910, edited by Joseph Meadon, the Republican Publishing Company, 1910.

Impressionist New York, William H. Gerdts, Abbeville Press, 1994.

The Graphic Arts and Crafts Year Book, 1911–12, edited by Walter L. Tobey, the Republican Publishing Company, 1912.

King's Handbook of New York City, Moses King, 1893.

King's Photographic Views of New York: A Souvenir Companion to King's Handbook of New York, Moses King, 1919.

The New New York: A Commentary on the Place and the People, John C. Van Dyke, illustrated by Joseph Pennell, the Macmillan Company, 1909.

New York, Ethel Fleming, illustrated by Herbert S. Kates, A&C Black, 1929.

New York: The Greatest City, F. W. Woolworth, New York.

New York: The Wonder City, American Art Publishing Company, 1919.

Our Society: Images and Stories from the Museum of the City of New York, Harry N. Abrams, Inc., 1997.

Picturesque America: A Delineation by Pen and Pencil, edited by William Cullen Bryant, D. Appleton and Company, 1874.

Portrait d'un Monde en Couleurs, Marc Walter and Sabine Arque, Solar, 2007.

The Real New York, Rupert Hughes, drawings by Hy. Mayer, the Smart Set Publishing Company, 1904.

Seeing New York: A Brief Historical Guide and Souvenir of America's Greatest City, American Sight-Seeing Coach Company, 1909.

United States Pictures, drawn by Richard Levett, the Religious Tract Society, London, 1891.

Victorian and Edwardian Fashions from La Mode Illustré, edited by Joanne Olain, Dover, 1998.

Views of Greater New York, Isaac H. Blanchard Company.

William Merritt Chase: Modern American Landscapes 1886–1890, Barbara Dayer Gallati, Brooklyn Museum of Art/Harry N. Abrams, Inc., 1999.

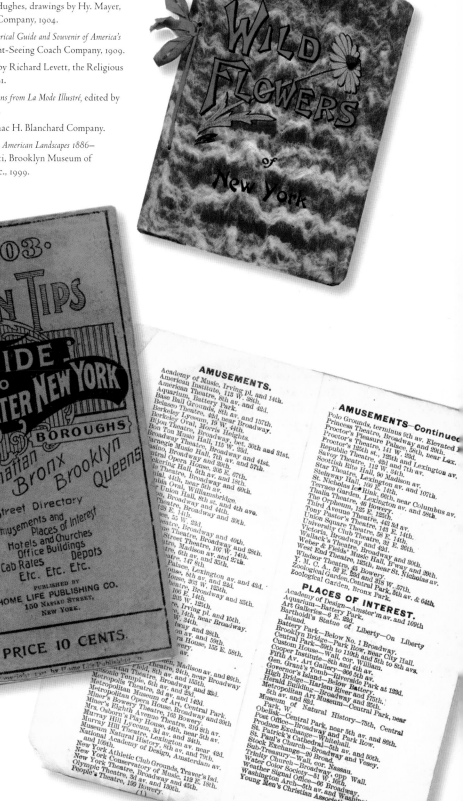

THE TIMES PAST ARCHIVE

The Memories of Times Past series would be inconceivable without the massive Times Past Archive, a treasury of books, magazines, atlases, postcards, and printed ephemera from the golden age of color printing between 1895 and 1915.

From the time several years ago when the project was first conceived, the collecting of material from all over the world has proceeded in earnest. As well as a complete set of the ninety-two A&C Black 20 Shilling color books, which are the inspiration for the series, the archive houses full sets of period *Baedeker* and *Murray's Guides*; almost every color-illustrated travel book from illustrious publishing houses like Dent, Jack, Cassell, Blackie, and Chatto & Windus; and a massive collection of reference works with color plates on subjects from railroads and military uniforms to wildflowers and birds' eggs.

The archive also contains complete runs of all the important periodicals of the time that contained color illustrations, including the pioneering *Arts and Crafts Year Book*; the first-ever color magazine, *Colour*; the journal *The Studio Illustrated*, which regularly included color sections; and full runs of American magazines that regularly featured color covers and plates, including *Century Magazine* and *Scribner's*.

These years were vintage years for atlas publishing, and the Times Past Archive contains such gems as Keith Johnston's *Royal Atlas of Modern Geography*, *The Harmsworth Atlas*, the Rand McNally *Library Atlas of the World*, and *The Philadelphia Enquirer's Pictorial Atlas of the Greater United States.*

Last but not least, the archive includes a wealth of smaller items—souvenirs, postcards, tickets, programs, catalogs, posters, and all the colorful ephemera with which the educated public of the age would have been familiar.

THE TIMES PAST WEB SITE

The Web site to accompany this project can be found at www.memoriesoftimespast.com, where you will find further information about the birth and development of the project, together with the complete original texts of titles published to date. There is also an area where you can take part in discussions raised by readers of the books who want to take their interest further and share their memories and passions with others. The Web site will start small and elegant, as you would expect of an "early twentieth-century Web site," but it will gradually become what you and we together make it, a place for devotees of art and culture from a century ago to meet and be inspired.

The Statue of Liberty, from *New York: The Wonder City*, The American Art Publishing Company, New York, 1919.